50 More Dinners in a Dash

*Sensational Three-Course Dinner Parties
in under 90 minutes*

Tessa Harvard Taylor

GRUB STREET • LONDON

Dedicated to my Mother, June

Acknowledgements

Where do I start? There are so many people to thank for helping this book come together. Let me start with Nick, my husband, for putting up with me over the last 13 years, but especially the weeks leading up to finishing this book when I have been talking about salsas, soufflés and satays in my sleep. For all his encouragement, support and tasting ability. To my twins, Jack and Katie who have helped test and taste recipes, their speciality being anything containing chocolate. To my Mother, who not only taught me to cook but whose help with proof-reading has been invaluable (she can't believe that I'm still as bad at spelling as I was when I was nine).

Anne Dolamore, my publisher, whose enthusiasm remains a constant inspiration, has been great fun to work with and for putting up with my weird sense of humour.

Thanks to two very special friends, Rebecca Michael and Billie Harris who have been a great source of inspiration when I have had "cookers cramp".

To Carol Bowen, Philip Langford, Sylvia Waller and Gaynor Oliver who have given professional advice.

To all the people who have helped with recipe testing and proof-reading, especially Fiona Boardman, Anne Alvis, Jane Hanson, Sue Bradbrook, Carey Botting, Jennie Pope, Susan Hall, Judy Reading-Kitchen, Liz Sansom, Lynville Barratt, Sue and Tony Grace, Carolyn Russell, Liz and Anthony Parkes, Nigel Barratt, Grasshopper Thompson, Jill Jennings, Moira McNally, Vicky Harvey, Jan Freemantle, Tricia Owen, Claire Walker, Barbara Rayner, Ann Davis, Lynn Riordan, Nisha Guihan and Michele Breene. Zue Newton but I'm not sure why!

Thanks to all the people who helped with the launch of my first book – Graham Mathews, Gareth Zundel, Keith Mason, Paul Thompson, Simon Jones, Jo Mealing, Mike Pucket, David Egan, Richard Groves and George Calton.

Gordon "Reg" Parris, Ashley "don't tell me you want it filleted again" and the team at Waitrose, Sunningdale.

Karen Wise from Oddbins who has recommended all the wines for this book.

Simon Smith and Alex Macdonald whose patience, sense of humour and professionalism made many hours of photography seem fun.

The White Lodge Centre for Living for helping to make me more computer literate.

Published by Grub Street
4 Rainham Close
London SW11 6SS

British Library Cataloguing in Publication Data
Taylor, Tessa Harvard
50 More Dinners in a Dash
1. Cookery 2. Quick and easy cookery
I. Title
641.5'55

ISBN 1 904943 13 6

Printed and bound by Replika Press Pvt. Ltd., India

Contents

Spring
15

ANGLING FOR A BITE
Asparagus and Mushrooms with a Puff Pastry Lid
Baked Trout in Chilli Oil with
Crispy Seaweed and Almonds
French Beans with Sesame Seeds
Potato and Tomato Bake
Lemon Mousse Tart with an Apricot Compote

RISOTTO IN A RUSH
Spinach and Ricotta Soufflé Cake with Cherry Tomato
and Walnut Compote
Oven-Baked Monkfish and Tiger Prawn Risotto
Fennel and Broad Bean Salad
Cinnamon Bruschetta with Brandy Marinated Fruit

EASTER ENTERTAINING
Filo Nests with Smoked Salmon, Quails' Eggs
and Dill Mayonnaise
Skewered Spring Lamb and Garlic with a Rosemary Sauce
Butter Bean Purée
Baby Spring Vegetables and New Potatoes
in a Mustard Dressing
Hot Cross Bun and Cinnamon Pudding

EASTERN PROMISE
Marinated Chilli Prawns and Fennel with Garlic Naan
Baked Salmon Stuffed with Lemon Grass, Ginger and Basil
Fish Noodles
Thai Roast Vegetables
Peanut Butter and Coconut Ice-Cream Terrine
with a Mango and Kiwi Salsa

VIRTUALLY FAT FREE
(Vegetarian Option)
Pea, Chilli and Ginger Soup with Onion Bagel Crisps
Basil Stuffed Chicken or Aubergine with Artichokes and
Yellow Peppers in a Balsamic Tomato Sauce
Tagliatelle Tricolore
Spinach and Bacon Salad with a Honey
and Mustard Dressing
Filo Tartlettes with Summer Fruit
and Marshmallows

FLORENCE BY CANDLELIGHT
Mushrooms Florentine with Dolcelatte and Ciabatta
Roast Tuna with a Tomato Pesto Crust
New Potatoes with Walnuts
Roast Aubergine and Pepper Salad
Summer Fruit and Amaretti Crumble
with Amaretto Cream

IN THE HOLIDAY MOOD
Seared Scallops with Spinach, Orange and Rocket
Turkey Fillets with Pesto, Prosciutto and Mozzarella
Green Tagliatelle
Broccoli with Garlicky Olive Oil
Lemon and Summer Fruit Tiramisu

ST PATRICK'S DAY

Smoked Trout and Horseradish Pâté with Warm Soda Bread
Beef, Wild Mushroom and Smoked Oysters
in Guinness with Puff Pastry Shamrocks
Irish Potato Cake
Roasted Root Vegetables with Thyme
Irish Coffee Pudding

SIMPLY RED

Spicy Salsa and Red Leicester Mini Tarts
Lamb Tagine with Apricots and Red Kidney Beans
Red Couscous
Beetroot, Tomato and Red Onion Salad
Summer Fruit and Mascarpone Cheesecake
with a Red Fruit Coulis

SHORT CUT CASSOULET

Chorizo, Couscous and Pine Nut Salad
Cassoulet of Seafood with Flageolet and Fennel
Gruyère Ciabatta Croutons
Braised Glazed Chicory
Individual Tarte Tatin with a
Maple Walnut Sauce

SICILIAN NIGHTS

Bresaola with Artichokes and Parmesan Shavings
served with Garlic and Basil Pizza
Salmon and Asparagus on a Bed of Ricotta-Filled Ravioli
Caramelised Red Onion and Blueberry Salad
Iced Tiramisu Terrine with a Marsala Sauce

BORDERING ON THE SWISS

Focaccia with Marinated Peppers,
Olives and Anchovies
Boursin Stuffed Chicken Breasts
Wrapped in Pancetta
Potato and Courgette Rösti
Sugar Snap Peas in Lemon Butter
Mocca Tarte with Grand Marnier Cream

Summer
48

ALFRESCO

Focaccia with Mascarpone and Sweet Onion Compote
Tapenade Stuffed Salmon with Marinated
Mediterranean Vegetables
Roast Tomato and Basil Salad
Tortellini and Rocket Salad
Summer Fruit Tartlettes

ORIENTAL BUFFET

Oriental Hors d'oeuvre with Thai Dipping Sauces
Thai Presidential Chicken
Wild Rice Salad with Basil and Sesame Oil
Broccoli and Almond Salad with an Oriental Dressing
Lime and Coconut Cheesecake

GRAB A CRAB

Garlic Mushrooms on Bruschetta
Gratin of Crab and Rocket
New Potatoes with Red Pesto
Spinach, Pancetta and Avocado Salad
Iced Coffee Meringue Cake with a Mocha Sauce

MACKEREL ON THE BARBECUE

Yellow Split Pea, Garlic and Basil Pâté
with Barbecued Bread
Barbecued Mackerel with Gremolata
B.L.T. Salad with a Ranch Dressing
New Potato Kebabs
Individual Iced Rhubarb Crumbles

4TH JULY

Mini Crispy Tarts with Pastrami and Dill Cucumber
Seared Tuna in a Tortilla Wrap with Corn and Mango Salsa
Caesar Salad with Anchovies and Parmesan Shavings
Sweet Potato Salad with a Parsley Dressing
Peanut Butter and Chocolate Cheesecake

MARRAKECH EXPRESS – BARBECUE

Spinach and Chick Pea Pâté with Eastern Flat Bread
Moroccan Spiced Lamb
Couscous with Pistachio Nuts and Coriander
Brandy Macerated Figs and Dates with Honeyed Yoghurt

A MOVEABLE FEAST

Asparagus in Prosciutto Wraps
Tuna and Sun-dried Tomato Fish Cakes
Wild Herb and Aioli Dip in a Bread Bowl
Green Crudités and New Potatoes
Citrus and Almond "Gunge" Cake with Fresh Strawberries

MYSTERY MUSTIQUE

Chilled Spicy Tomato, Clam and Celery Soup
with Warm Corn Chips
Swordfish with Cajun Spices and a Kiwi and Cucumber Salsa
Green Bean, Banana, Cashew and Coconut Salad
Stuffed Baked Sweet Potatoes
Sweet Tortilla Shells with Pineapple and Malibu Ice Cream

NO COOK INDIAN

Prawn, Avocado and Mango with Poppadoms
Chicken Tikka and Lime Kebabs with a Spinach and Mint Raita
Curried Lentils and Bulgur Wheat
Carrot, Sultana and Coriander Salad with an
Orange and Ginger Dressing
The Amazing Banana Pavlova

A PENNE FOR YOUR THOUGHTS
(Vegetarian)

Asparagus with Black Olive Tapenade and Garlic Bread Sticks
Penne Pasta with Roast Vegetables,
Pine Nuts and Chèvre
Artichoke and Borlotti Bean Salad
Iced Lemon Meringue and Vodka Mousse

A SMART SUPPER IN ADVANCE

Warm Courgette Timbales with Red Pepper Marmalade
Three Salmon Kedgeree with Wild Rice
and Quails' Eggs
Cherry Tomato and Watercress Salad with an
Elderflower Dressing
Double Bourbon Iced Terrine with Raspberries and a
Maple Pecan Sauce

TRULY TROPICAL

Avocado and Red Kidney Bean Dip with Tortilla Chips
Tropical Fish Stew with Coconut Milk in Melon Bowls
Brown Rice with Blackeye Beans
Melon and Cucumber Salad in a Lime and Chive Dressing
Baked Bananas in Rum with Cinnamon Ice Cream

VEGETARIAN BARBECUE

Sweet Onion and Harissa Jam Tarts
Marinated Halloumi, Apricot and Courgette Kebabs
Chargrilled Pepper and Chick Pea Salad
Bulgur Wheat with Cucumber, Coriander and Pumpkin Seeds
Tortilla Pancakes with Pistachio, Sultanas and a Caramelised
Orange Sauce

Autumn
85

BLACK THAI

Mini Seafood Spring Rolls with a Sweet Chilli Sauce
Baked Thai Green Chicken
Oriental Crunch Salad
Seven Spice Rice Timbales
Toffee Fondue with Exotic Fruit

GOOD COD – A Wheat and gluten-Free Feast

Polenta and Pesto Pizzas with Sun-dried Tomatoes
and Gorgonzola
Roast Cod in a Parmesan Crust with a Red Pepper, Caper
and Black Olive Compote
Sweet Potato Bake
French Beans in Walnut Oil
Chocolate Amaretti Cake with Praline Ice Cream

BEIJING BANQUET

Noodle Nests with Crab and Spring Onion
Fish and Oyster Mushroom Spring Rolls
with a Black Bean Sauce
Coconut Rice
Chinese Vegetable Salad with a
Sweet and Sour Dressing
Crispy Rice Cakes with Ginger,
Pawpaw and Chinese Gooseberries

DAIRY-FREE DUCK

Prawns with a Bloody Mary Salsa
Duck Legs with a Confit of Caramelised Onion and Pear
Celeriac and Mustard Mash
Roast New Potatoes with Orange and Thyme
Filo Baskets with Blackberries, Cassis and Blackcurrant Sorbet

OLD FAVOURITES

Egg Mayonnaise with Anchovies and Sun-dried
Tomatoes on Croutons
Scallop, Prawn, Mussel, Smoked Cod and Spinach Pie
Topped with Gruyère Rösti
Beetroot with Marmalade
Treacle, Kumquat and Ginger Tart

DINNER IN HALF THE TIME

Spinach, Prawn and Lemon Grass Soup
Duck with Ginger, Orange and Black Bean Sauce
Oriental Sesame Vegetables with Noodles
Hot Spiced Rice Pudding with Lychees and Mango

NO FUSS FRENCH

Mussel Soup
Roast Poussin with Lemon, Garlic and Tarragon
Gratin of New Potatoes with Raclette
Roast Vegetable Ratatouille
Crêpes with Apples and Raisins in Calvados

CONTEMPORARY ITALIAN

Spinach and Dolcellate Soufflé
Pork Pizzaiola with Pepperoni
Gnocchi with Pesto
Balsamic Broccoli
Passion Fruit and Marshmallow Seduction

JAPAN IN A DASHI

Suburban Sushi
Teriyaki Salmon with Water Chestnuts
Roast Japanese Vegetables with Ginger
Rice Noodles with Sesame Oil
Exotic Sticky Fruit Pancakes

PLEASURES OF PROVENCE

Salad of Endive, Lardons and Brioche Croutons with
a Warm Goats Cheese Dressing
Stuffed Toulouse Chicken with a Walnut Sauce
Roast Provençal Tomatoes
New Potatoes in Garlic and Wine
Feuilleté with Prunes in Armagnac and
Crème Pâtissière

HEY PESTO

Globe Artichoke with Warm Red Pepper Hollandaise
Salmon and Pesto Fish Cakes with a Bulgur Wheat Crust and
Tomato, Caper and Basil Salsa
Microwave Risotto with Wild Mushrooms
and Red Onions
Broad Bean and Radicchio Salad
Nectarine and Raspberry Mascarpone Gratin

VEGETARIANS OF THE ORIENT

Oriental Roast Vegetable Satay on Poppadoms
Thai Quorn Curry with Coconut and Mango
Basmati Rice with Mint and Cumin
Stir-fry Broccoli and Baby Corn with Sesame Seeds
Iced Banoffi and Banana Terrine with a Rum and
Butterscotch Sauce

Winter
121

A DINNER PARTY FOR THE AGA

Grilled Aubergine and Halloumi Cake with a
Spicy Cucumber Dressing
*Mustard and Ginger Marinated Lamb Medallions ****
Orange, Pine Nut and Raisin Pilaff
Roasted Root Vegetables with Coriander
Pear and Almond Tart

HALLOWEEN

Leek and Broccoli Soup with Roquefort Croutons
Devilled Pork Medallions
Chilli and Coriander Mash
Roast Pumpkin with Cinnamon and Brown Sugar
Turte a l'Orange

BUBBLY BRUNCH

Steaming Hot Bloody Mary Soup with
Warm Cheese Straws
Smoked Haddock with a Béarnaise Sauce
Cashew Nut Risotto
Red Cabbage, Apple and Caraway Salad
Spiced Cider Fruit Compote with Yoghurt and
Blueberry Muffins

CANCUN COOKING

Tortilla Baskets with Prawn, Avocado and Tomato Salsa
Venison Chilli with Crème Fraîche and Coriander
Roast Sweet Corn and Red Onions
Cheesy Baked Potato Wedges
Banana, Mango, Fudge and Rum Brulée

PERFECT POT ROAST

Leek and Stilton Crumble
Pot Roast Guinea Fowl with Pancetta on a Bed of
Barley Risotto with Wild Mushrooms
Red Cabbage in Mulled Wine
Flapjack Tart with Apple, Pecan and Ginger

FINGER FOOD IN A FLASH

Mini Bagels with Smoked Salmon and Cream Cheese
Mexican Crudités
Pizza Squares with Spinach and Chèvre
Marinated Mozzarella, Cherry Tomatoes and
Black Olives
Sun-dried Tomato and Puff Pastry Pinwheels
Berry Berry Punch

GOOD GAME

Baked Chèvre with Lime Marinated Sultanas on Muffins
Mixed Game Cassoulet with Apples and Cider ****
Couscous
Courgettes with Mustard
Sticky Toffee Banana Mille-Feuille

CONSUMING PASSION

Puff Pastry Hearts with Asparagus Spears
in Hollandaise Sauce
Intercourse of Lemon Sorbet in Champagne
Herb Stuffed Plaice on a Double Bed of Roasted Red
and Yellow Peppers
Pasta Beaus with Pesto
Passion Fruit and Pineapple Syllabub

LOSING POUNDS WITH PANACHE

Butternut Squash and Orange Soup
Turkey, Mushroom and Red Pepper Strogoulash
Green Herbed Bulgur Wheat
Balsamic Leeks with Wholegrain Mustard
Hot Raspberry Ramekins

INSTANT INDIAN FROM THE STORE CUPBOARD

Spicy Red Lentil Soup with Poppadoms
Prawn, Cod and Chick Pea Masala
Lemon and Saffron Rice
Spinach with Tomato, Ginger and Cumin
Mango and Cardamom Kulfi with Pistachio Nuts
and Cinnamon ****

THANK GOODNESS IT'S NOT TURKEY

Smoked Haddock and Leek Timbales with a
Lemon and Chive Dressing
Roast Gammon with Kumquats and a Honey,
Mustard and Soy Glaze ****
Puy Lentils with Red Onion
Celery and Hazelnut Crumble
Clafoutis with Cherries in Kirsch with
White Chocolate Ice Cream

CAREFREE CHRISTMAS

Crostini with Smoked Wild Venison
Cranberry Stuffed Turkey Fillets Wrapped in Bacon
with a Stilton Sauce
Carrot, Parsnip and Ginger Purée
Potato and Onion Cake
Christmas Roulade with a Brandy Mac Sauce

CHRISTMAS LEFT-OVERS

Pear, Celery and Walnut Salad with a
Warm Stilton Dressing
Left-overs with a Mushroom Sauce in Puff Pastry Cases
Bubble and Squeak Cakes
Carrots in Honey and Cinnamon
Christmas Pudding Syllabub with Biscotti

Foreword

Times have changed so much over the past few decades. Just to give you an idea, 50 years ago a housewife would spend an average of 18 hours per week cooking compared to 7 hours per week in the late 1990's. Even though life is easier in some ways, it's not surprising that so many people have less time for cooking, trying to juggle jobs, children, housework, sport, and a bit of relaxation. Socialising and entertaining so often get forgotten but with all the modern aids such as microwaves, food processors, convenience foods and, of course, "Dinners in a Dash" there's no need to put entertaining at the bottom of your list of priorities.

I started "Dinners in a Dash" in the form of cookery demonstrations, creating recipes to show people how to prepare and cook an elegant three course dinner in under two hours. This is done using a combination of fresh natural ingredients, "instant" products, such as couscous, egg noodles, filo pastry, jars of pesto and other high quality convenience foods, not to mention a bit of cheating! The demonstrations proved so popular that I decided to compile a book of my recipes, and so *Dinners in a Dash* was published in 1996.

I have no formal cooking qualifications but a huge amount of experience in instant entertaining. I worked as a "Chalet Cook" in ski resorts, in villas in Greece and on a Kibbutz in Israel where the less time spent in the kitchen meant more time skiing or on the beach. I now lead a busy life combining children (I have 9 year old twins, Jack and Katie), work, entertaining and trying to find time to go to the gym, to work off some of the excess calories I have consumed while testing all my recipes (250 in total) for this book. This is why, like so many people, I need quick easy recipes which give the impression that I have spent hours, if not days, making them!

Even though my last words having finished my first book were "never again" I find myself having completed this, my second book. It's amazing how memories fade. People started to ask me when the next would be published. They'd cooked every recipe in the book three times over and wanted new ones. There were demands from friends and clients for even quicker recipes, more Oriental and Italian menus and even more that can be prepared in advance. Gradually I found myself mentally creating new recipes which led to testing them out just in case I decided to write another book. Nick, my husband, started to become suspicious when he found himself eating three variations of the same dish. So here is *50 More Dinners in a Dash*, with even quicker menus to create in under 90 minutes.

Here's what the papers said about my first book:

"DINNERS IN A DASH IS IDEAL FOR BUSY WOMEN WHO ENJOY ENTERTAINING."
The Daily Mail

"TESSA BELIEVES THAT LIFE IS TOO SHORT TO BE TIED TO THE KITCHEN. HER PHILOSOPHY IS TO CHEAT WITH FLAIR AND CONFIDENCE TO CREATE IMPRESSIVE AND EXCITING FOOD. YOUR GUESTS WILL THINK YOU'VE SPENT WEEKS PORING OVER COOK BOOKS AND SLAVISHLY FOLLOWING COMPLICATED RECIPES."
Good Housekeeping

"IF YOUR DINNER PARTIES TAKE AT LEAST A DAY TO PREPARE, GET A COPY OF TESSA HARVARD TAYLOR'S BOOK.
Ideal Home Magazine

"FASCINATING INFORMATION AND INSPIRING IDEAS."
Chic Magazine

If you already own a copy of my first book, I'm sure you will enjoy my new selection of innovative and even faster menus. For you first time "Dinners in a Dashers" I hope you will find the book interesting, stimulating, daring, and it will enable you to actually enjoy entertaining.

If you would like details of my cookery demonstrations write to :
Dinners in a Dash, Kenwolde Manor, Callow Hill, Virginia Water, Surrey GU25 4LF.

I shall be donating 10% of all royalties to The Centre for Living, White Lodge Centre, Holloway Hill, Chertsey, Surrey – a day centre for people with disabilities.

Tessa Harvard Taylor

INTRODUCTION

NO NEED FOR MENU PLANNING

All the recipes in the book are set out as complete dinner party menus. This saves you the laborious task of pouring over recipes working out which starter goes with which main course, vegetables, etc. However, feel free to experiment and 'mix 'n match' courses to suit your mood. The menus are grouped into seasons, using seasonal produce, but in most cases there is no reason why you can't swap them around and cook a spring menu in winter for example. Some of the menus have certain themes, e.g. "Eastern Promise", "Truly Tropical", "Carefree Christmas", "Simply Red". Even though these menus include some typical dishes and ingredients, they are not necessarily genuinely authentic. Authenticity often takes time and these recipes are designed to save time. Many factors have been taken into account when planning menus. For example, colour, oven space, time, "cheatability", calorific value. On the subject of calories, I have mentioned where it is possible to use "low-fat" alternatives but in some cases, it just tastes so much better to use the "full fat" version. If you are using these recipes for everyday cooking, then it may be a good idea to use as many low-fat substitutes as possible, but for special occasions when entertaining guests, it shouldn't matter if you have a few extra calories.

All the recipes are for eight people but they can easily be doubled, halved or, even better, if you are cooking for only four, you can follow the recipes for eight and, where appropriate, freeze half.

AHEAD OF TIME

Most of the recipes can be prepared in advance or frozen. It will indicate in the recipe at which stage this can be done.

The following symbols apply:

❄ May be frozen

◑ May be made the day before

☼ May be made earlier in the day

Where a recipe can be made in advance, it should be cooled, covered and refrigerated unless otherwise stated.

All menus can be prepared in 90 minutes or less but where you see a **** symbol, this indicates that something in the menu needs marinating, cooking or freezing for longer than 90 minutes.

WINE

Wines, recommended by Oddbins, are given with each menu to save you even having to think about what to drink. Most of the wines are priced between £5-£7 a bottle but a few special ones are slightly more expensive. I have suggested a style of wine with each menu, such as a peppery and fruity red and then a particular named wine, such as, Mount Hurtle Old Vine Grenache from Australia, but you can also make your own choice.

SHOPPING

This can be a real chore but you should be able to find everything under one roof if you shop at a large supermarket. If it means going miles out of your way to buy the suggested brands, then don't bother. They are only recommendations and there will probably be other good brands more easily available that you can use. Where a recipe mentions fish or meat to be filleted and skinned, get the fishmonger/butcher/supermarket to do it for you – don't waste time doing it yourself.

CONVERSIONS from metric to imperial are not strictly accurate but are rounded up or down to make the recipes easier to follow. Where a quantity is given in "ml" (millilitres) it will be virtually the same in "g" (grams) and can be converted accordingly. Metric and imperial quantities may be mixed in my books.

COOKING TIMES – all cooking times are given assuming you are using the quantities for 8 people. If you are using smaller or larger quantities, you may have to adjust the cooking time accordingly, i.e. less time for smaller quantities and more time for larger quantities.

EGGS – recipes have been tested using medium sized eggs. No raw eggs have been used in any of the recipes due to possible health risks.

FAN ASSISTED OVENS – reduce temperature by 10°. For best results refer to manufacturer's handbook.

FROZEN FOOD – make sure food has cooled completely before putting it in the freezer. Always defrost before cooking unless otherwise stated. Allow plenty of time for de-frosting – I recommend taking food out of the freezer the day before it is needed and de-frosting in the fridge overnight until needed.

FRUIT PLATTER – I recommend serving a fruit platter with the dessert. This means that your guests have an alternative if they prefer not to eat the pudding. It takes far less time than a fruit salad, looks attractive and your guests can just help themselves with their fingers. See seasonal platters opposite page 16.

HERBS – in the recipes, I talk about handfuls In most cases, the amount you use is a matter of taste. If you prefer to be more precise then follow the rule that 1 handful = 2 tablespoons. Use fresh herbs whenever possible, but if not, use one quarter of the quantity if using dried herbs.

MARINATING – only marinate food in non-metallic dishes. Where a recipe tells you to marinate before cooking, either do this in a non-metallic oven-proof dish or marinate in a bowl and transfer to a roasting tin before cooking.

MICROWAVES – all timings have been worked out on a 650 watt oven. When microwaving, bowls should be covered with cling-film, leaving a gap for steam to escape. As a general rule, the food being microwaved should be stirred half way through cooking.

PREPARATION OF INGREDIENTS – all recipes are quick and time saving. Unless a recipe tells you to peel a potato, tomato, etc. – don't do it – it's not necessary and just a waste of time.

QUANTITIES – there is no need to weigh everything out to the last milligram. Where possible, I talk about handfuls, tablespoons, slugs, etc. as the amount you use is a matter of taste.

SPOON MEASURES – all spoon measures are level unless otherwise stated.

HANDY HINTS AND TIME SAVERS

BREAD – tastes so much better when served warm. This is a trick I learnt years ago. Damp the bread with water, wrap in silver foil and put in a medium oven for 10 minutes. Even day old bread tastes and smells as if it has been freshly baked.

BREADCRUMBS – if you have stale bread, put it in a food processor to make breadcrumbs and store in freezer. They can be used straight from the freezer when needed.

BURNT CASSEROLES – to take the burnt taste away, add a cube of chocolate and stir in until melted – it may seem unlikely but it works.

CAKES AND TARTS – where a recipe for a tart or cheesecake is cooked in a spring-form of loose-bottomed tin, you should remove the side of the tin before serving but do not remove the base unless you are going to freeze it. If so, the tart or cheesecake can be removed when frozen by sliding a palate knife between the base of the tin and the cake or tart. It can then be returned to the freezer or placed on a serving plate to de-frost.

CHILLING – to speed up the process of chilling or setting cheesecakes, mousses, pâtés, etc, put in freezer for first 30 minutes then transfer to fridge. For chilled soups, add a few ice cubes.

CHILLIES – take care when handling them. The real fiery heat is in the seeds so make sure you remove all of them. Wash you hands well immediately after handling chillies. If you prefer, you can always substitute a few drops of chilli sauce or Tabasco for the real thing.

CHOCOLATE – when melting chocolate take care as it can sometimes scorch. There are two ways of doing this: 1. Break chocolate up into a bowl and set over a saucepan of hot (not boiling) water until it melts. 2. Break chocolate up into a bowl, cover with cling – film, leaving a gap for steam to escape and microwave on medium for time mentioned in recipe or until melted. Stir half way through cooking. It is better to melt it too gradually rather than too quickly. The chocolate tends to keep its shape, so you will have to stir it with a spoon to see if it has melted enough. Chocolate melted in a microwave will go solid again quickly so you will have to use it straight away after melting.

CONVENIENCE INGREDIENTS – some of the convenience ingredients I have used can only be obtained from large supermarkets or specialist delis. I suggest you buy them when you see them and store for when they are needed. Certain items can be frozen, e.g. tubs of ready-made cheese or mushroom sauce, ready-rolled puff pastry, etc.

CRUSHING BISCUITS AND MERINGUE – a quick way of doing this is to transfer them to a well sealed bag, drop on the floor, and gently tread on them until crushed. Make sure the bag doesn't break open!

DRESSINGS – there are many ready-made salad dressings on the market. It is a matter of finding the one you like best but I recommend Marks and Spencer's "95% Fat Free French Dressing" which is my favourite and it's low in fat. It has a long shelf life so I stock up with a few bottles whenever I go to M & S.

DRESSING SALADS – with most salads it's important that they are not tossed in dressing until just before serving, otherwise they go soggy. To save time and washing up, when making your own dressing, you can mix it in the bottom of the salad bowl, put the salad servers crossed over on top of the dressing, and the salad resting on the servers. Toss together at the last minute.

EGGS – when separating eggs, if a bit of yolk falls into the white by mistake, the easiest way to remove it is to scoop it out with half an egg shell. The whites may not whisk stiff enough if any of the yolk remains. Always whisk egg whites first and then the yolks – this means you won't have to wash the whisk in-between. A test to see if egg whites are whisked enough, is to turn the bowl up-side-down after whisking. If they stay in the bowl they are fine, if they fall out, it means they are not whisked enough!!

FILO PASTRY – so many people are put off by reading the complicated instructions on the packet. Don't – just follow my instructions. Buy fresh filo if you can, it is much easier to handle than frozen. There is no need to take it out of the fridge two hours in advance and no need to cover it with a damp tea towel (as stated in the instructions). As long as you don't leave it lying around for ages, it won't dry up. Handle it gently, but if it does rip, don't panic! Most recipes will require about four layers of filo, so make sure the ripped piece is not on the top and it won't be noticed.

FREEZING FOOD - where a recipe may be frozen, make double quantities and freeze half. This will mean that you have an instant dish when entertaining in the future.

FRESH CONVENIENCE FOODS – if you have problems finding certain fresh ingredients, e.g. fresh Napoletana sauce, fresh cheese sauce, they also come in long life jars which will work just as well.

LOW-FAT – alternative to butter – I recommend "Olivio" which you can use to cook and it tastes good.

MISTAKES – never, ever confess if something has gone wrong. Just make a few alterations if possible and pretend it's the way it's meant to look. For example, you are making the Mocha Tart with Grand Marnier Cream, you forget to take the tart out of the oven and the top gets burnt. Simply scrape the burnt top part off and dust heavily with icing sugar. If it is really bad, then spread the Grand Marnier Cream on top of the tart. See more tips in individual recipes.

ONIONS WITHOUT TEARS – there are many different theories about chopping onions, but I find the only fool-proof method is to light a candle and keep it near the onion – sounds strange but it really does work.

PASTRY – it should be chilled between preparing and cooking it. To speed up the process, put prepared pastry in the freezer for 10 minutes instead of "chilling for 1 hour" as other recipe books will tell you to do.

SAUCES THAT CURDLE – if the hollandaise or béarnaise sauce curdles because it has been heated too quickly, assuming you have some spare sauce, stir it in and it will stop the curdling.

SHOPPING LISTS – don't make them – just take a copy of 50 more Dinners in a Dash with you.

THICK SAUCES – if a sauce becomes too thick – add some wine to thin it down.

VEGETABLES – if you worry about having to cook vegetables at the last minute and feel you've got to stand over the saucepan to make sure they don't go soggy, stop worrying. Here are a couple of suggestions to alleviate your worries. Cook vegetables in advance, but for slightly less time than indicated, drain and put in a non-metallic serving dish. Cover with cling-film, leaving a gap for steam to escape, and put in microwave for a few minutes before serving to heat them up. Serve straight from the microwave. The other alternative is to forget about vegetables and serve a salad instead.

ZESTING – There is quite an art to zesting so I

suggest, for first timers, you buy a spare lemon to practise on. Hold the zester at an angle close to the lemon and pull down hard. Fine strips of rind should appear. I far prefer zesting the rind of fruit rather than grating it.

EQUIPMENT

Here are some items which I feel are necessary for speed and presentation:

CAKE TIN – round spring-form or loose bottomed – approx. size 24cm (9½″) in diameter.

CASSEROLE – large oven-proof – at least 2.5 litres (4½ pints) in capacity.

ELECTRIC WHISK – for quickly whisking egg whites, cream, etc.

FOOD PROCESSOR – absolutely essential for short-cut cooking. Use for chopping, slicing, grating, puréeing, etc. It is incredibly time saving, especially when ingredients are processed in the right order so that you don't have to clean it out each time, e.g. chop herbs first, grate cheese second and purée vegetables third without washing it up in between. See more tips in individual recipes.

GARLIC CRUSHER – the quickest way of mashing garlic. You can now buy self-cleaning ones which push the bits of garlic out from both sides.

GRATIN OR SHALLOW OVEN-PROOF DISH – 2.25 litres (4 pints) in capacity.

KEBAB STICKS – metal or wooden. If you buy metal ones, get the flat type which make turning easier. When using wooden ones, soak them in water for an hour to stop them burning.

KNIVES – you will probably already have your own favourite knives but it is very important to keep them sharp; it enables you to work more quickly and make a neater job.

LEMON SQUEEZER AND ZESTER – through zesting the skin of lemons and oranges you save yourself the pain of grating your fingers!

MICROWAVE – also extremely time saving. Can be used for de-frosting, re-heating, melting chocolate, etc. You can also cut down on washing up by microwaving food in the dish in which it will be served.

PLATTERS – a large round serving platter or two – at least 30cm (12″) in diameter. They are always useful for arranging fruit, serving tarts, cold main courses, etc. They can either be made of china or glass.

PYREX BOWLS – 1 litre (1¾ pints) and other sized Pyrex bowls are useful. The dishes are handy when marinating and to cook food in.

RAMEKIN DISHES – at least 8. If you are buying new ones, get the ones without gold rims so that they can go in the microwave.

RE-USABLE BAKING PARCHMENT – "Bake-O-Glide". Available by mail order from Falcon Products, Scott House, 43 Scott Avenue, Baxenden, Accrington, Lancs BB5 2XA

ROASTING TINS – the larger the better. I would recommend vitreous enamel. They are available at good kitchen shops and some supermarkets.

ROULADE TINS – same as a Swiss roll tin – approx. size 30cm x 22cm (12″ x 8½″). I recommend vitreous enamel – it is very hard wearing and easy to clean.

SERVING BOWLS – large and decorative. Useful for salads, hot vegetables, couscous, etc

12 – HOLED TART/MUFFIN/BUN TINS   vitreous enamel recommended.

TART TIN – large, loose-bottomed – approx. 28cm (11″) in diameter.

TERRINE DISH – which will hold 1.5 litres (2½ pints)

WOK – very useful when stir-frying large quantities.

USEFUL STORE CUPBOARD INGREDIENTS

You will find that you have to buy fresh ingredients every time you have a dinner party, but here are some useful items to keep in your cupboard, fridge or freezer:

Bacon-flavoured soya bits
Biscuits – amaretti, digestive, gingernut
Bulgur Wheat
Capers
Chocolate
Couscous
Custard – long-life in cartons
Dressings for salads – "M & S 95% Fat Free French Dressing" recommended
Dried fruits – apricots, pears, prunes, sultanas, raisins, dates, figs
Fish soup – in jars "Select Marée" recommended
Flour – plain
Fruit purées – apricot and rhubarb – "Bonne Maman" recommended
Garlic – fresh
Honey – any type
Lentils – red
Marmalade
Mayonnaise
Meringue – ready-made in packets
Mushroom – dried wild and in jars marinated in oil
Mustard – French and wholegrain
Noodles
Nuts – cashew, pecan, pine, walnut, hazelnuts, pistachios, almonds (flaked and ground)
Oils – extra virgin olive, walnut, sesame, ground nut
Olive paste – black
Passatta – creamed tomatoes
Pepper – black peppercorns for grinding
Peppers – marinated in jars
Pasta – dried penne or other shapes
Peanut butter
Pesto – in jars
Pizza bases
Polenta
Poppadoms
Potatoes – long life packets or rösti
Rice – long-grain and wild, Thai, Basmati, risotto
Sea salt – ground
SAUCES:
　Béarnaise sauce – in jars
　Black bean sauce – "Sharwoods" recommended
　Butterscotch sauce – "Smuckers" recommended
　Chilli sauce
　Chocolate sauce
　Curry type sauce – "Tilda Madhur Jaffrey" Green Lime Masala recommended

Dill mustard sauce
Fish sauce
Hollandaise sauce – in jars
Maple syrup
Pasta sauce in jars, e.g. "Loyd Grossman", "Ragu", "Dolmio" or supermarket own brand – Waitrose "Pasta Sauce, Original Tomato" recommended
Soy sauce
Spicy tomato salsa – "Pace" recommended
Toffee sauce – "Smuckers" recommended
Worcester sauce
SEEDS:
　Pumpkin seeds
　Sesame seeds
Stock cubes – chicken, lamb, fish and vegetable
Sugar – brown, granulated, caster, icing
Sun-dried tomatoes – in oil and paste
Tapenade – black and green olive
TINNED:
　Anchovies
　Artichoke hearts
　Black olives
　Beans – blackeye, butter beans, flageolet, chick peas
　Cannellini beans
　Chopped tomatoes
　Coconut milk
　Lentils
　Lychees
　Mango
　Milk – condensed and evaporated
　Tomato juice
Vinegar – ordinary wine, balsamic
HERBS AND SPICES
It is better to buy fresh herbs and spices when needed but here are some dried ones which are worth keeping a stock of: –
　Allspice
　Caraway seeds
　Cardamom pods
　Cinnamon – ground
　Chinese 5 spice
　Coriander – ground
　Cumin seeds
　Curry powder – mild
　Dried mixed herbs
　Ginger
　Green Thai curry paste
　Lemon grass
　Nutmeg
　Paprika

Saffron
Thai 7 spice
Turmeric
ITEMS FOR THE FRIDGE:
　Butter and "Olivio"
　Crème fraîche
　Eggs – medium
　Fromage frais
　Milk
　Parmesan
ITEMS FOR THE FREEZER:
　Bread – ciabatta, baguette, focaccia, naan, tortillas, other types
　Fish – cod steaks
　Fruit – raspberries and mixed summer fruit
　Ice cream – good quality vanilla, mango sorbet
　Pastry – short crust, puff and ready-rolled puff pastry. The ready-rolled is usually sold fresh but can be kept in the freezer at home
　Prawns
　Sauces – fresh ready-made tubs of cheese or mushroom sauce – sold at most large supermarkets, usually near the fresh pasta. They can be frozen and are handy to keep to de-frost for emergencies
　Stock – chicken, lamb, vegetable – sold fresh in cartons, can be kept in the freezer at home and de-frosted when needed
　Vegetables – spinach and broadbeans
ALCOHOL:
　Amaretto
　Brandy
　Cassis
　Cointreau
　Marsala
　Red and white wine (also handy for the odd drink while cooking)
　Sherry
　Sickly sweet fruity liqueur which you can buy on holiday in Spain, Portugal, etc. (this will probably only be suitable to cook with as it will be too revolting to drink!)
　Vodka
　Whisky

ANGLING FOR A BITE

*T*his is a lovely fish menu which contains no shellfish, making it ideal for non-meat eaters, Jewish friends and others who don't eat shellfish.

ASPARAGUS AND MUSHROOMS WITH A PUFF PASTRY LID

I was recently asked to go to a charity lunch at the Dorchester Hotel. Not only did I enjoy myself but I was inspired to create this recipe based on the chef's starter.

Cut off the rough end of the asparagus, cut each stalk in half and plunge into boiling water for 5 minutes until tender. Drain and mix with sliced mushrooms, asparagus soup, wine and season. Divide mixture between 8 ramekin dishes.

Unroll the pastry and cut into 8 circles, 8.5cm (3¼") in diameter. Place pastry on top of ramekins and push to seal down the outside.

◖ May be prepared up to this point the day before.

Put into oven for 15 minutes and serve.

200g (7oz) small fresh asparagus tips

250g (9oz) chestnut
mushrooms – sliced

1 tin Campbell's condensed
asparagus soup

1 glass dry vermouth or white wine

1 packet (375g) ready-rolled
puff pastry

salt and pepper

Oven: 190°C, 375°F, Gas Mark 5

BAKED TROUT IN CHILLI OIL WITH CRISPY SEAWEED AND ALMONDS

I have used fillets in this recipe as a great many people are put off eating trout because of all the bones.

Mix olive oil with chilli, garlic, salt and pepper. Pour over trout and leave to marinate for at least 30 minutes.

◖ May be prepared up to this point the day before.

Place trout with marinade and almonds on a baking tray and put in oven, uncovered for 20 minutes. Put seaweed on top and put back in oven for a further 3 - 5 minutes and serve.

Cook's tip: Crispy seaweed is now available from most large supermarkets. It is actually cabbage with spices to give the effect of seaweed. It's shredded finely and tends to burn easily so don't leave it in the oven for any longer than 5 minutes.

---

4 tbsp olive oil

1 red chilli – de-seeded and finely
chopped or 2 tsp chilli sauce

2 cloves garlic – crushed

8 whole trout fillets

1 packet (100g) flaked almonds

2 packets (40g each) crispy seaweed –
see Cook's tip below

salt and pepper

Oven: 190°C, 375°F, Gas Mark 5

FRENCH BEANS WITH SESAME SEEDS

The addition of just a small amount of sesame oil and seeds gives the beans a wonderfully nutty flavour and texture.

Top and tail beans and cook in boiling water for about 10 minutes or until tender. Drain. Return to the pan and add olive oil, sesame seeds, salt and pepper. Toss over heat for 1 minute and serve.

1kg (2lbs 4oz) French beans

1 tbsp sesame or olive oil

50g (2oz) sesame seeds

salt and pepper

POTATO AND TOMATO BAKE

1.5kg (3lbs 5oz) potatoes – scrubbed and diced into squares about 1cm (½")

2 tins (400g each) chopped tomatoes with herbs

2 cloves garlic – chopped or crushed

salt and pepper

Oven: 190ºC, 375ºF, Gas Mark 5

This potato dish is cooked and served in the same dish and looks best cooked in a heavy, rustic pottery dish.

Put potatoes in a large gratin dish or flattish, oven-proof serving dish or dishes. Add other ingredients. Cover with foil and cook in oven for 1 ½ hours.

◑ May be made the day before.

To re-heat – put in oven for 30 minutes.

LEMON MOUSSE TART WITH AN APRICOT COMPOTE

300g (10 ½oz) ginger nut biscuits

85g (3oz) butter – melted

300ml (½pt) double cream

1 tin (400g) condensed milk

2 lemons – zest and juice

1 jar (600g) apricot compote – "Bonne Maman" recommended

The inspiration for this recipe came from my days in Greece. I used to make something called "Lemon Bicci Pudding" made with evaporated milk as cream was very expensive. I have adapted it and used double cream which makes it fluffier and more mousse-like.

Crush the biscuits (may be done in a food processor) and mix with melted butter. Press into the bottom and up the sides of a loose bottomed tart tin or flan dish approx. 28cm (11") in diameter. Put in fridge while preparing the filling. Mix the condensed milk and lemon zest and juice together. Whisk the cream until thick and fold into the condensed milk mixture. Pour into prepared tin and put back in fridge for at least 1 hour.

◑ May be made the day before.
❋ May be frozen.

Serve with apricot compote.

Cook's tip: You can make compote yourself by putting a tin of drained apricots into a food processor and pulsing.

ORDER OF PREPARATION IF MAKING IN ADVANCE:

The day before:
1. Prepare and cook potatoes.
2. Make starter.
3. Marinate trout.
4. Make lemon tart.

In the evening:
5. Prepare beans and cook as needed.
6. Re-heat potatoes as necessary.
7. Cook starter.
8. Cook trout and seaweed.

ORDER OF PREPARATION IN UNDER 90 MINUTES:

1. Prepare and cook potatoes.
2. Make tart.
3. Prepare trout and cook as needed.
4. Make starter.
5. Prepare and cook beans as necessary.

Opposite: Seasonal Fruit Platters,

Top Left: – Spring (grapes, melon, kiwi fruit)

Top Right: – Winter (star fruit, physalis, lychees)

Bottom Right: – Summer (watermelon, cherries, strawberries)

Bottom left: – Autumn (figs, passion fruit, dried pears)

RISOTTO IN A RUSH

♀ A full flavoured, toasty
Chardonnay.
Recommendation – Vinas del Vero
Barrel Fermented Chardonnay
from Spain

*A*t a glance, this menu looks complicated, with recipes like soufflés
and risottos which need to be cooked at the last moment. Well it
isn't, and in fact both these recipes can be prepared in advance and need
no last minute stirring or dash to the table in case the soufflé sinks.

SPINACH AND RICOTTA SOUFFLÉ CAKE WITH CHERRY TOMATO AND WALNUT COMPOTE

This is a cross between a cake and a soufflé. The beauty of it is that it
can be made the day before and re-heated. You can use chopped or leaf
spinach in this recipe, both taste delicious but the cake will be easier to
cut if you use the chopped variety.

oil for greasing
3 thsp grated Parmesan
500g (1lb 2oz) frozen chopped or leaf spinach – de-frosted
500g (1lb 2oz) ricotta
5 eggs
salt and pepper
COMPOTE
24 cherry tomatoes – cut in half
100g (3½oz) walnut pieces
1 tbsp balsamic vinegar
2 tbsp walnut oil
1 tsp sugar
salt and pepper
Oven: 190°C, 375°F, Gas Mark 5

Grease a spring-form cake tin, 24cm (9½") in diameter, with oil and sprinkle
Parmesan over the base and around the sides. Separate the eggs and mix the
yolks with spinach, ricotta and season generously. Whisk egg whites until stiff
and fold into spinach mixture. Put into cake tin and cook in oven for 30
minutes. Mix compote ingredients together. Remove the sides of cake tin and
serve soufflé cake with the compote, either warm or cold.

◑ May be prepared the day before.

To re-heat – put soufflé back in oven for 15 minutes to warm through and
serve with compote.

Cook's tip: The compote is best when served warm. Just heat gently.

FENNEL AND BROAD BEAN SALAD

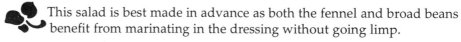

This salad is best made in advance as both the fennel and broad beans
benefit from marinating in the dressing without going limp.

500g (1lb 2oz) frozen broad beans
4 fennel bulbs
8 tbsp ready-made French dressing
salt and pepper

Cook the broad beans according to instructions on the packet and toss in
dressing while still hot. Discard the base and any tough outer leaves of the
fennel and slice. Toss together with broad beans and season.

☼ May be made earlier in the day.

*Opposite: Virtually Fat Free,
vegetarian option (page 25)*

OVEN BAKED MONKFISH AND TIGER PRAWN RISOTTO

 I absolutely adore risotto but I hate the thought of standing over a risotto pan for half an hour, adding one ladle of stock at a time and getting hot and steamy. This risotto cooks in the oven while you are eating your starter, so you can remain cool, calm and relaxed with your guests.

Heat the oil in a large flame-proof casserole or saucepan. Add the leeks, peppers and garlic and sauté gently for 5 minutes. Add the rice and stir to coat with oil.

✳ May be prepared up to this stage earlier in the day.

Add wine and soup. Fill empty soup jar with water (800ml) and add to the pan. Bring up to the boil and simmer for 10 minutes, stirring occasionally. Add monkfish and prawns, and transfer to the oven for 30 minutes. Season and serve with basil and lemon wedges.

Cook's tip: There are some excellent fish soups around these days. The ones in jars are the best and I would recommend "Select Marée" or Waitrose own brand.

3 tbsp olive oil

2 large leeks – sliced

2 red peppers – de-seeded and sliced

2 garlic cloves – sliced

500g (1lb 2oz) risotto rice

300ml (½pt) white wine

1 jar (800ml) good quality fish soup (see Cook's tip)

500g (1lb 2oz) monkfish – boned and cut into cubes

500g (1lb 2oz) uncooked, shelled tiger prawns

2 handfuls chopped basil

2 lemons – cut into wedges

salt and pepper

Oven: 190°C, 375°F, Gas Mark 5

CINNAMON BRUSCHETTA WITH BRANDY MARINATED FRUIT

I have fond memories of my Grandmother making cinnamon toast – it was a real treat. This is a variation of the same thing but with a sophisticated twist.

Peel pineapple, core and cut into chunks. Remove the stones from the apricots and plums and slice. Mix fruit with brandy and orange juice.

◗ May be prepared up to this stage the day before.

Spread butter over each slice of ciabatta and sprinkle brown sugar and cinnamon on top. Put under a pre-heated grill for 3 minutes or until golden and bubbling. Serve with fruit.

Cook's tip: Other fruit may be used instead, e.g. peaches, mango, pawpaw.

1 small pineapple

8 apricots

8 plums

4 tbsp brandy

150ml (¼pt) orange juice

1 ciabatta – cut into 8 thick slices

25g (1oz) butter

4 tbsp brown sugar

2 tsp cinnamon

ORDER OF PREPARATION IF MAKING IN ADVANCE:

The day before:
1. Make soufflé cake up to ◗
2. Prepare and marinate fruit.

Earlier on the day.
3. Make risotto up to ✳
4. Make salad.

In the evening:
5. Re-heat soufflé cake.
6. Cook risotto.
7. Make bruschetta.

ORDER OF PREPARATION IN UNDER 90 MINUTES:

1. Marinate fruit and prepare bruschetta – put under grill just before serving.
2. Make soufflé cake and compote.
3. Make risotto.
4. Make salad.

EASTER ENTERTAINING

*E*aster is a great time for entertaining and with so many wonderful spring ingredients to choose from, it's not too difficult. The filo nests with quails' eggs look festive, lamb is at its best at this time of the year and as for the pudding – well, you can't have Easter without hot cross buns. If you have children, you could prepare an Easter egg hunt, and remember, the more mini eggs you plant around the garden, the more peace and quiet you will have to prepare this menu.

FILO NESTS WITH SMOKED SALMON, QUAILS' EGGS AND DILL MAYONNAISE

1 packet fresh filo pastry – or 8 sheets (measuring approx 30cm x 18cm/ 12" x 7")
2 tbsp olive oil
16 quails' eggs
6 tbsp mayonnaise – the low fat type may be used
2 handfuls chopped dill plus a few sprigs for decoration
juice and zest of half a lemon
150g (5oz) smoked salmon
salt and pepper
Oven: 180°C, 350°F, Gas Mark 4

Life's too short to peel a quail's egg – and that's exactly why I haven't in this recipe. They look much prettier in their shells and it gives your guests something to do!

Lay one sheet of filo out and lightly brush half of it with oil and fold in ½ to form a square. Cut the square in half and half again. You will now have 4 squares. Brushing in-between with oil, lay the second square on top of the first at an angle so you have an 8 pointed star (each will have 4 layers of filo). Put in tart, deep bun or muffin tins and brush top of tarts with oil. Repeat this process until you have 16 tarts. Cook in oven for 10 minutes until golden. Leave to cool.

Put the quails' eggs into cold water, bring up to the boil and allow to cook for 3 minutes. Once cooked, plunge into cold water. Mix the mayonnaise with chopped dill, zest and juice of half a lemon, salt and pepper.

◑ May be prepared up to this point the day before.

To serve – allow two tarts per person. Put a blob of mayonnaise on one side of each tart. Cut the smoked salmon into 16 pieces, curl each piece and put on the other side of the tart. Put a sprig of dill on top and two quails' eggs beside the tarts.

Cook's tip: Explain to your guests that they will need to peel the quails' eggs and they can be dipped in the dill mayonnaise.

SKEWERED SPRING LAMB AND GARLIC WITH A ROSEMARY SAUCE

16 lamb loin chops

16 garlic cloves

3 handfuls fresh rosemary

2 tbsp olive oil

1 tub (200ml) crème fraîche

300ml (½pt) lamb stock
(see Cook's tip below)

salt and pepper

Oven: 220°C, 425°F, Gas Mark 7

There is nothing nicer at this time of the year than sweet, tender spring lamb and there is nothing that goes better with lamb than rosemary and garlic. These lamb chops are simply baked in the oven with the garlic, left in its skin, which can then be squeezed out over the lamb.

You will need 8 thin metal skewers or wooden kebab sticks. Wrap an unpeeled garlic clove inside each lamb chop and stick the skewer through the chop and garlic, allowing two chops and two garlic cloves per skewer. Put in a non-metalic dish, add olive oil, 1 handful of the rosemary, salt and pepper and leave to marinate for at least 30 minutes or until ready to cook.
Chop remaining 2 handfuls of rosemary and put in a saucepan with crème fraîche, stock, salt and pepper. Bring up to boil and then allow to simmer for 30 minutes to reduce.

◑ May be prepared the day before.

Put lamb on a rack over a roasting tin and cook in oven for about 30 minutes, turning half way through (cook for less time if you like your lamb pink and more if you like it really well done). Re-heat the sauce over a gentle heat for about 5 minutes. Serve lamb on top of a pool of butter bean purée (see recipe) with the sauce served separately.

Cook's tip: Either buy a carton of fresh lamb stock or make it with boiling water and half a lamb stock cube. You will also need extra for the butter bean purée.

BUTTER BEAN PURÉE

3 tins (420g each) butter beans

2 garlic cloves

4 tbsp olive oil

150ml (¼pt) lamb stock

salt and pepper

These large cream coloured beans are puréed to give a slightly sweet, velvety finish – delicious with lamb.

Put all ingredients in a food processor until smooth.

◑ May be prepared up to this stage the day before.

Put in a saucepan over a gentle heat for 10 minutes or put in a microwave on high for 5 minutes. Serve with lamb.

BABY SPRING VEGETABLES AND NEW POTATOES IN A MUSTARD DRESSING

1.3kg (3lbs) new potatoes

1.3kg (3lbs) baby vegetables – choose a mixture of some of the following: asparagus tips, baby corn, baby carrots, French beans – topped and tailed, dwarf courgettes or patty pans

MUSTARD DRESSING

2 tsp wholegrain mustard

2 tbsp olive oil

1 tbsp balsamic vinegar

salt and pepper

Spring is the time for lovely sweet baby vegetables. Not only do they look pretty but they take no time at all to prepare. In this recipe they are cooked together with the potatoes, so you will need one very large saucepan, and it will save on the washing up afterwards.

Scrub or wash vegetables. Cook potatoes in boiling water for 10 minutes, then add baby vegetables for around 7 minutes and drain. Mix mustard dressing ingredients together. Return vegetables to the pan and add dressing. Toss together over a gentle heat for 1 minute and serve.

HOT CROSS BUN AND CINNAMON PUDDING

8 hot cross buns

75g (3oz) butter or "Olivio"

2 handfuls raisins or sultanas

2 tins (425g each) custard

1 tbsp cinnamon

2 tbsp brown sugar

Oven. 170°C, 325°F, Gas Mark 3

If you think of bread and butter pudding as real comfort food, you'll find this pudding so comfortable you could fall asleep!

Slice each bun vertically into 4 or 5 and butter one side of each slice. Grease a large shallow oven-proof dish and lay them, butter side up, slightly overlapping in the dish. Scatter the raisins on top, followed by the custard, cinnamon and brown sugar.

◑ May be prepared up to this stage the day before.

❊ May be frozen at this stage.

Put in oven, uncovered, for 1 hour.

Cook's tip: It is always a good idea to buy double the amount of hot cross buns as I find that half of them get eaten before you even get round to preparing this recipe.

ORDER OF PREPARATION IF MAKING IN ADVANCE:

The day before:
1. Make starter up to ◑
2. Make butter bean purée up to ◑
3. Make pudding up to ◑
4. Prepare lamb.

In the evening:
5. Prepare baby vegetables and make mustard dressing
6. Finish off starter.
7. Cook lamb and heat butter bean purée as needed.
8. Cook vegetables.
9. Cook pudding.

ORDER OF PREPARATION IN UNDER 90 MINUTES:

1. Prepare starter and assemble before eating.
2. Prepare lamb and butter bean purée and cook as necessary.
3. Prepare vegetables and mustard dressing and cook as necessary.
4. Prepare pudding and put in oven when needed.

EASTERN PROMISE

♀ *Wine: A very rich, ripe white. Recommendation – Mariquita from California*

*E*astern and Oriental cooking is so popular these days and all the ingredients needed to make the recipes are now more readily available. The only snag with Oriental cooking is that so much of it has to be prepared and cooked at the last minute, so I have created this menu where most of it can be prepared the day before. There is very little to do on the day, so you can have a relaxing evening with your guests – and that's a promise.

MARINATED CHILLI PRAWNS AND FENNEL WITH GARLIC NAAN

500g (1lb 2oz) large, cooked, peeled prawns – de-frosted if frozen

1 green pepper – chopped

2 heads of fennel – sliced

1 red chilli – finely chopped

2 garlic cloves – chopped

2 handfuls chopped coriander

4 tbsp olive oil

2 limes

salt and pepper

4 large garlic naan or 8 small naan

This dish lends itself to the wonderful large tiger prawns that you can buy either fresh or frozen. They absorb all the delicious flavours of the other ingredients while marinating and the addition of green pepper and fennel gives a real crunch.

Mix prawns with green pepper, fennel, chilli, garlic, coriander, olive oil, juice of ½ a lime and season. Leave to marinate for at least 1 hour or preferably over night.

◗ May be prepared up to this stage the day before.

Wrap naan in foil and put in oven: 200°C, 400°F, Gas Mark 6 for 15 minutes to warm.

Cut remaining lime into slices and serve with marinated prawns and warm naan.

Cook's tip: Take great care when chopping chillies. Remove stalk and all seeds and rinse under cold water. Chop finely and wash hands thoroughly when finished.

BAKED SALMON STUFFED WITH LEMON GRASS, GINGER AND BASIL

1 whole salmon (approx. weight
2.25kg (5lbs) – ask supermarket or
fishmonger to fillet and skin it –
alternatively buy 2 salmon fillets
(approx. total weight 1.3kg (3lbs))

1 jar "Bart Spices" fresh lemon grass
(see Cook's tip below)

3cm (1 ¼") cube fresh root ginger –
peeled and chopped

2 handfuls shredded basil

3 lemons

salt and pepper

Oven: 200ºC, 400ºF, Gas Mark 6

I dislike a whole salmon sitting on a plate staring at me and having to struggle with head, bones and skin when serving it but as it's more economical to buy a whole salmon, I ask the supermarket or fishmonger to fillet and skin it for me. You still have to check for stray bones before cooking it but at least when it comes to serving , all you have to do is slice it into 8 portions. The salmon is also delicious served cold.

Mix together lemon grass, chopped ginger, shredded basil, juice of 1 lemon and season. Check all bones have been removed from the salmon, spread the mixture over one fillet and place the other fillet on top. Wrap in foil to seal.

◗ May be prepared the day before.

Place salmon on a baking tray and cook in foil in oven for 45 minutes. Cut remaining lemons into wedges and serve with the salmon

Cook's tip: Barts lemon grass comes in jars already chopped. If you cannot find it, buy 3 fresh lemon grass stalks and chop them finely.

FISH NOODLES

2 packets (250g each) medium egg
noodles

4 tbsp sesame or olive oil

6 tbsp fish sauce (nam pla)

 These noodles are cooked and simply tossed in oil and fish sauce. Fish sauce is the Thai equivalent of soy sauce and gives a wonderful flavour.

Cook noodles according to instructions on packet, drain and toss in oil and fish sauce.

◗ May be cooked the day before.

To re-heat – Put in microwave on high for 5 minutes, stirring half way through.

To serve salmon and noodles – either put noodles on a large platter and place whole salmon on top or cut salmon into 8 portions and serve on a bed of noodles on individual plates.

Cook's tips: If re-heating, you may need to add another tablespoon of oil if the noodles dry out. Soy sauce may be used instead of fish sauce.

THAI ROAST VEGETABLES

6 courgettes – sliced on the diagonal

300g (10½oz) baby carrots – scrubbed

250g (9oz) baby corn

8 spring onions – cut in half
on the diagonal

1 jar "Sharwoods Basil and Chilli Thai
Stir Fry" (see Cook's tip)

2 tbsp sesame or olive oil

Oven: 200°C, 400°F, Gas Mark 6

I like to use yellow courgettes for this recipe as they look so bright and vibrant. If you can't get them, use the green ones instead.

Mix all ingredients together and put in a roasting tin. Cook in oven for 1 hour, tossing half way through.

Cook's tip: Other types of stir-fry sauces may be used with these vegetables.

PEANUT BUTTER AND COCONUT ICE-CREAM TERRINE WITH A MANGO AND KIWI SALSA

1 litre good quality vanilla ice cream

1 (400ml) tin coconut milk

3 heaped tbsp crunchy peanut butter

SALSA

1 large ripe mango

4 kiwi fruit

large slug (approx 4 tbsp) fruity
liqueur e.g. Cointreau, Grand Marnier

The thought of peanut butter in ice cream may make you squirm, but try it and I guarantee you'll be pleasantly surprised. It has a lovely refreshing combination of flavours to end a spicy meal.

Allow ice cream to soften slightly. Line a 1.5 litre (2¾pt) terrine or loaf tin with foil. Mix ice cream with coconut milk and peanut butter, put into the prepared terrine tin and return to freezer for at least 2 hours.

To make salsa – peel mango, cut flesh off the stone and chop. Peel kiwi and chop. Mix fruit with liqueur.

◑ The salsa may be made the day before.

❋ The terrine may be kept in a freezer for up to 2 months.

To serve – lift ice cream out of terrine dish, put on a serving plate and remove foil. Keep in fridge for half an hour before serving. Slice and serve with salsa.

Cook's tip: For an even quicker dessert, you could serve the salsa with plain vanilla ice cream or bought mango sorbet.

ORDER OF PREPARATION IF MAKING
IN ADVANCE:

The day before:
1. Marinate prawns.
2. Prepare salmon recipe up to ◑
3. Cook noodles.
4. Make ice cream terrine and salsa.

In the evening:
5. Prepare vegetables and put in
   oven as needed.
6. Cook salmon as required.
7. Warm naan in oven.
8. Re-heat noodles
9. Transfer terrine from fridge to freezer
   30 minutes before serving.

ORDER OF PREPARATION IN UNDER
90 MINUTES:

1. Make ice-cream terrine and salsa.
2. Marinate prawns.
3. Prepare and cook vegetables.
4. Prepare and cook salmon.
5. Warm naan in oven.
6. Cook noodles.

VIRTUALLY FAT FREE
(Vegetarian Option)

♀ A fruity rose.
Recommendation – Bloody Good
Rose from California

The best way to lose weight is to cut down on fats and this is also important for people with high cholesterol but there's no reason why low fat means boring. This virtually fat-free menu proves that light, healthy eating can be a real delight.

All the recipes are suitable for vegetarians apart from the chicken which can be substituted with aubergine.

PEA, CHILLI AND GINGER SOUP WITH BAGEL CRISPS

1.7 litres (3 pts) vegetable stock – made with 3 stock cubes and boiling water

1 large bag (2kg) frozen peas

2 onions – roughly chopped

3cm (1¼") cube fresh root ginger – peeled and roughly chopped

2 tsp chilli sauce

2 tsp cumin seeds

salt and pepper

½ a red pepper

4 bagels

Traditionally peas have been a summer vegetable, but these days, as most people buy frozen peas, they can be eaten all year round. I think peas make wonderful soups and the great advantage of this recipe is that it can be served hot for a chilly Spring evening or chilled if the weather is warmer.

Put all ingredients except red pepper and bagels in a large saucepan and bring up to the boil. Simmer for 15 minutes. Blend in a liquidizer or food processor until smooth.

◐ The soup may be made the day before.

✳ May be frozen.

To make bagel crisps, cut bagels horizontally into 4 thin rounds. Either put under a pre-heated grill for approximately 40 seconds on each side or put on a baking tray in oven: 190°C, 375°F, Gas Mark 5 for 5 minutes on each side until golden.

Either serve soup chilled or re-heat in a saucepan over a gentle heat until piping hot.

To serve: Finely chop the red pepper. Pour soup into bowls and sprinkle red pepper on top. Serve with warm bagel crisps.

Cook's tip: If you think the soup is too thick, you can add skimmed milk to thin it down a little.

BASIL STUFFED CHICKEN OR AUBERGINE WITH ARTICHOKES AND YELLOW PEPPER IN A BALSAMIC TOMATO SAUCE

8 skinless chicken breasts (or 4 large aubergines for vegetarian option – see Cook's tip)

4 handfuls basil – reserve a few leaves for decoration

3 cloves garlic – chopped or crushed

1 tin (400g) artichoke hearts – drained and cut in half

2 yellow peppers – stalk and seeds removed and thickly sliced

2 jars (680g each) Passata (or creamed tomatoes)

4 tbsp balsamic vinegar

salt and pepper

Oven: 190ºC, 375ºF, Gas Mark 5

It's amazing that a dish with such wonderful flavours can be thrown together so easily.

Cut slits in the chicken breasts and open out like a book. Place basil leaves and garlic down the centre of each and fold up. Place in an oven-proof dish, slit side down. Add all other ingredients apart from basil leaves for decoration.

◖ May be prepared up to this point the day before.

Cover with foil and cook in oven for 1¼ hours basting occasionally. Decorate with remaining basil leaves and serve with pasta.

Cook's tip: Alternative recipe for vegetarian option: Substitute 4 large aubergines for the chicken. Cut the stalks off the tops of the aubergine and slice them lengthways into 6 pieces, approx. 1cm (½") thick. Drop the slices into a large pan of boiling water and blanch for 3 minutes (you may have to do this in two or three batches). Drain well and dry on kitchen paper. When the aubergine slices are cool enough to handle, place the basil and garlic at the wider ends of the slices, season and roll up. Place tightly in an oven-proof dish with the overlapping ends facing down. Follow recipe as for chicken but only cook for 1 hour.

TAGLIATELLE TRICOLORE

500g fresh tagliatelle tricolore or white and green pasta

salt

Tagliatelle tricolore is flat pasta in three colours, white, green and red, and produces a beautifully colourful contrast when served.

Cook according to instruction on packet. Serve with basil stuffed chicken or aubergine.

Cook's tip: Even though this pasta cooks in 4 minutes, it's a drag to have to cook it in between courses. Here is a tip for cooking it just before sitting down to the first course. Bring the water up to boil, plunge in the pasta, bring back up to the boil, turn off heat and leave to stand in water with the lid on the pan. Drain when ready to serve.

SPINACH AND BACON SALAD WITH A HONEY AND MUSTARD DRESSING

2 bags (200g each) baby spinach leaves

6 tbsp bacon flavour soya chips – "Betty Crocker Bacos" recommended

8 tbsp ready-made fat-free dressing – "Provender Fat Free Honey and Mustard Dressing" recommended

Since when did bacon become fat-free and vegetarian? Well it hasn't but the soya bacon bits used in this recipe are suitable for vegetarians, virtually fat-free and the second best thing since bacon.

Toss all ingredients together.

Cook's tip: If you dress a salad too early it will go soggy but what you can do is put the dressing in the bottom of the salad bowl, lay the salad servers on top crossed over and put the spinach and soy bacon bits on top. Toss just before serving.

FILO TARTLETTES WITH SUMMER FRUIT AND MARSHMALLOWS

1 packet fresh filo pastry – or 16 sheets

500g (1lb 2 oz) frozen summer fruit

*1 packet (200g) marshmallows
(see Cook's tip below)*

icing sugar for dusting

*3 small tubs (125g each) vanilla or
fruit flavoured virtually fat-free
yoghurt*

Oven: 180°C, 350°F, Gas Mark 4

It seems so many people are terrified of using filo pastry. Well this will show you just how easy it is and you'll be sure to receive plenty of compliments. Unlike other types of pastry, filo is very low in fat but this is usually increased, in most recipes, by the addition of melted butter. My recipe, however, needs no melted butter or oil and it tastes just as good.

You will need one or two 12-holed deep tart or muffin trays. Take one sheet of filo, and fold in half lengthways. Cut in half to form two rectangles. Cut each rectangle in half and lay one on top of the other at an angle to form a star shape. You should now have the bases of two tarts each with 4 layers of filo. Place in tart/muffin tray and repeat process until you have 16 tarts. You may have to do this in two batches if you have only one tart tray. Cook in oven for 10-15 minutes until golden. Leave to cool.

Prepare filling – put frozen fruit in a saucepan with the marshmallows and heat gently until the marshmallows have melted. Allow to cool.

◗ May be prepared up to this point the day before.

Put yoghurt into a small serving bowl for people to help themselves. Just before serving, fill the filo tartlettes with fruit and marshmallow mixture and dust with icing sugar.

Cook's tip: If you are making this for a vegetarian, make sure the marshmallows you buy are suitable for vegetarians – available from most health food shops

ORDER OF PREPARATION IF MAKING IN ADVANCE:

The day before:
1. Make soup.
2. Prepare stuffed chicken/ aubergine up to ◗
3. Make filo tarts up to ◗

In the evening:
1. Put chicken/aubergine in the oven.
2. Prepare salad.
3. Make bagel crisps.
4. Cook tagliatelle.
5. Fill filo tarts just before serving.

ORDER OF PREPARATION IN UNDER 90 MINUTES:

1. Make soup and leave to cool.
2. Prepare and cook stuffed chicken / aubergine as needed.
3. Make filo tarts and prepare filling.
4. Prepare salad.
5. Make bagel crisps.
6. Cook tagliatelle.
7. Fill filo tarts just before serving.

FLORENCE BY CANDLELIGHT

♀ *A fruity Italian white.*
Recommendation – Bidoli Sauvignon
Blanc from Italy

I dreamt up this menu while spending a weekend in Florence with my husband. After busy days sightseeing we spent wonderful romantic evenings relaxing on the banks of the river Arno having candle-lit dinners and drinking fine Italian wine.

MUSHROOMS FLORENTINE WITH DOLCELATTE AND CIABATTA

They say "life's too short to stuff a mushroom" – but not when you use my recipe.

500g (1lb 2oz) frozen spinach – de-frosted
8 very large or 16 medium mushrooms
125g (4½oz) cream cheese with garlic and herbs – "Philadelphia" recommended
125g (4½oz) dolcelatte
1 garlic clove
olive oil
salt and pepper
1 ciabatta
Oven: 190ºC, 375ºF, Gas Mark 5

Wipe the mushrooms and remove the stalks. Drain the de-frosted spinach and mix with cream cheese, season and stuff inside the mushrooms. Cut dolcelatte into thin slices and place on top.

◗ May be prepared up to this point the day before.

Either put mushrooms on a baking tray in oven for 20 minutes, or put under a hot grill for 5 - 7 minutes until hot through. Put ciabatta in oven according to instruction on packet. Slice into 16 pieces (allowing 2 per person) and serve with mushrooms on top.

Cook's tip: I would recommend cooking the mushrooms in the oven if you have room, rather than under the grill, as you can then use the liquid they produce to pour over them.

ROAST TUNA WITH A TOMATO PESTO CRUST

Tuna tends to be a very dry fish and it is important not to overcook it. Cooked this way with the tomatoes and pesto, they add moisture to make it a deliciously succulent dish.

8 tuna steaks (approx 175g (6oz) each)
1 tub (190g) fresh pesto
4 tomatoes – chopped
4 heaped tbsp brown breadcrumbs (made from 1½ slices bread)
2 lemons
basil leaves for decoration
salt and pepper
Oven: 190ºC, 375ºF, Gas Mark 5

Mix pesto with chopped tomatoes, juice of 1 lemon, salt and pepper. Spread mixture on top of tuna steaks.

◗ May be prepared up to this stage the day before.

Place tuna on a baking tray, sprinkle breadcrumbs on top and cook in oven for 25 minutes. Cut remaining lemon into wedges and serve with tuna, juices from the pan and decorate with basil leaves.

Cook's tip: If you like your tuna rare in the middle then cook it for a few minutes less.

NEW POTATOES WITH WALNUTS

The addition of walnuts and walnut oil to new potatoes metamorphoses them into something deliciously nutty.

1.5kg (3lbs 5oz) new potatoes
100g (3½oz) walnut pieces – chopped
2 tbsp walnut oil
salt and pepper

Cook the potatoes in boiling, salted water until tender – about 15 minutes. Drain and toss in remaining ingredients.

ROAST AUBERGINE AND PEPPER SALAD

I love roast vegetables and find them so versatile as they can be served hot or cold in a salad or sandwiched between fresh crusty bread.

2 large or 3 medium aubergines – sliced

2 red and 2 yellow peppers – de-seeded and cut into 6

2 garlic cloves – chopped

8 tbsp olive oil

3 tbsp balsamic vinegar

200g (7oz) mixed salad leaves

salt and pepper

Oven: 220°C, 425°F, Gas Mark 7

Put the aubergines, peppers and garlic in a large roasting dish, toss in 4 tbsp oil and season.

Put in oven for 40 minutes. Toss in remaining oil and balsamic vinegar while hot and leave to cool.

◗ May be prepared up to this point the day before.

Put salad leaves into a large salad bowl and toss in aubergine and pepper mixture.

SUMMER FRUIT AND AMARETTI CRUMBLE
WITH AMARETTO CREAM

Amaretto is a delicious Italian liqueur made out of almonds. If you don't have a bottle you could use another liqueur.

1kg (2lbs 4oz) frozen mixed summer fruit

1 packet (250g) Amaretti biscuits

300ml (½pt) whipping cream

large slug (approx 4 tbsp) Amaretto or other liqueur such as Grand Marnier or Cointreau

2 tbsp icing sugar

Oven: 180°C, 350°F, Gas Mark 4

If you are making this recipe the day before, there is no need to de-frost the summer fruit. Put summer fruit in a large oven-proof serving dish or gratin dish. Crush Amaretti biscuits and put on top of fruit. Add Amaretto and icing sugar to cream and whisk until thick.

◗ May be prepared up to this point the day before.

Put crumble in oven for 30 minutes and serve with Amaretto cream.

Cook's tip: As an alternative to Amaretto cream, the crumble could be served with yoghurt, crème fraîche or ice cream.

ORDER OF PREPARATION IN MAKING IN ADVANCE:

The day before:
1. Prepare mushrooms.
2. Prepare tuna up to ◗
3. Prepare roast vegetables up to ◗
4. Prepare crumble up to ◗.

In the evening:
5. Cook mushrooms and warm ciabatta as needed.
6. Cook tuna and potatoes as needed.
7. Toss roast vegetables into salad leaves.
8. Put crumble in oven.

ORDER OF PREPARATION IN UNDER 90 MINUTES:

1. Prepare and cook roast vegetables up to ◗. Toss together with leaves just before serving.
2. Prepare mushrooms and cook as necessary. Warm ciabatta in oven.
3. Prepare tuna and cook as necessary.
4. Cook potatoes as needed.
5. Prepare and cook crumble.

IN THE HOLIDAY MOOD

♀ A crisp, lively Italian.
Recommendation – Gavi la
Chiara from Italy

*H*ave you ever had friends round for dinner to decide where you're going for your next holiday? This menu, with recipes and flavours of the Mediterranean, will get you in the mood for holiday planning. Even if you are not planning a holiday, you can still enjoy these dishes.

SEARED SCALLOPS WITH SPINACH, ORANGE AND ROCKET

3 oranges

6 tbsp olive oil

600g (1lb 5oz) Queen scallops

200g (7oz) baby spinach leaves

2 handfuls fresh rocket – chopped

Salt and pepper

This starter is served cold. The scallops are first cooked and, while still hot, mixed with an orange dressing, allowing them to soak up all the delicious tangy flavours.

Take the zest of two of the oranges and mix with the juice of one. Peel the remaining two, slice and cut the slices in half. Add 5 tbsp of the olive oil and season generously.

Add remaining 1 tbsp olive oil to a frying pan and heat until oil begins to smoke. Add scallops and cook over intense heat for 2 minutes, tossing half way through. Add hot scallops to orange mixture and leave to cool until ready to serve.

◑ May be prepared up to this stage the day before.

Arrange spinach leaves on 8 individual plates, followed by scallop and orange mixture and chopped rocket leaves sprinkled on top. Serve with ciabatta, focaccia or other Italian bread.

Cook's tip: King scallops may also be used but should be cut in half before cooking.

TURKEY FILLETS WITH PESTO, PROSCIUTTO AND MOZZARELLA

16 small thin turkey fillets or
8 large ones

½ jar (85g) pesto – red or green

8 slices prosciutto

2 packets (125g each) mozzarella –
cut into 16 slices

2 jars (440g each) "Ragu" sauce or
other pasta sauce

2 handfuls fresh basil

Oven: 190°C, 375°F, Gas Mark 5

Why is it we only think of eating turkey around Christmas? It's available all year round, inexpensive and can be used in so many different ways. This recipe combines it with many flavours of the Mediterranean.

Put turkey fillets in one layer in an oven-proof dish. If using 8 large fillets, cut them in half. Spread with pesto, put half a slice of prosciutto on top and then a slice of mozzarella. Pour "Ragu" sauce on top and scatter over 1 handful of shredded basil.

May be prepared up to this point the day before.

Cook in oven for 45 minutes. Decorate with remaining basil leaves and serve.

GREEN TAGLIATELLE

500g (1lb 2oz) fresh green tagliatelle

Plain tagliatelle is delicious and all you need to go with the rich flavours of the turkey dish.

Cook as instructions on packet.

Cook's tip: Other types of pasta can be used with this menu.

BROCCOLI WITH GARLICKY OLIVE OIL

1.3kg (3lbs) broccoli

1 garlic clove – crushed

1 tbsp olive oil

salt and pepper

I love fresh broccoli but the addition of garlic and olive oil make it even more delicious.

Cut thick stalks off broccoli and break up into florets. Add to boiling, salted water and cook for 6 - 8 minutes. Drain and toss in crushed garlic and olive oil.

Cook's tip: I prefer this freshly cooked but if you would rather cook it in advance, it should be cooked for slightly less time than stated above and put in a microwave to re-heat before serving.

LEMON AND SUMMER FRUIT TIRAMISU

1 tub (250g) mascarpone

1 tub (400ml) fresh custard

1 Madeira cake (250g) – usually sold as a block

4 tbsp Marsala, Madeira or sweet sherry

zest and juice of 1 lemon

500g (1lb 2oz) frozen Summer fruit – no need to de-frost

1 tbsp icing sugar

Tiramisu is similar to Coronation chicken. The connection is that they've both been rather "over-done" but most people have to confess that they secretly still really enjoy them. So, due to Tiramisu's great popularity, I have come up with a lovely tangy Summer version. There's no need to de-frost the fruit before making this recipe as the fruit will de-frost in the pudding allowing all the wonderful juices to soak into the Madeira cake.

Mix mascarpone with custard (don't worry if there's the odd lump). Slice the Madeira cake into about 12 thin slices and lay half the slices in the bottom of a serving bowl. Pour half the Marsala and lemon juice (reserve the zest for decoration) over the cake, followed by half the Summer fruit and spread half the mascarpone/custard mixture on top. Repeat the same process – cake, Marsala, lemon juice, fruit, mascarpone mixture and sprinkle lemon zest on the very top. Leave at room temperature for 2 hours before serving to allow the Summer fruit to de-frost. Dust with icing sugar and serve.

◐ May be made the day before

Cook's tip: The Tiramisu looks effective served in a glass bowl so that you can see all the different layers or alternatively can be served in individual glasses.

ORDER OF PREPARATION IF MAKING IN ADVANCE:

The day before:
1. Make scallop recipe up to ◐
2. Make turkey recipe up to ◐
3. Make tiramisu up to ◐

In the evening:
4. Cook turkey, broccoli and pasta as needed.
5. Assemble starter.

ORDER OF PREPARATION IN UNDER 90 MINUTES:

1. Make tiramisu.
2. Make scallop starter.
3. Make turkey recipe and cook as necessary.
4. Cook broccoli and pasta as necessary.

Opposite: Simply Red (page 36)

ST. PATRICK'S DAY

♀ *A full, fruity Sauvignon.*
Recommendation – Villa Maria,
Private Bin Sauvignon Blanc from
New Zealand
A warm, spicy Côtes du Rhônes.
Recommendation – Côtes du Rhône
Parallèle 45 Paul Jaboulet Ainé
from France

I have had many holidays in Southern Ireland and enjoyed the beautiful countryside and extremely friendly people. I was also very impressed with the food – a real mixture of local produce and international cuisine which I have tried to reflect in this menu.

2 lemons
300g (10½ oz) smoked trout fillets
400g (14oz) cream cheese – the low fat type may be used
3 tbsp creamed horseradish
2 handfuls fresh dill
2 lemons
pepper
1 – 2 loaves soda bread

SMOKED TROUT WITH HORSERADISH PÂTÉ AND WARM SODA BREAD

This is really a cross between a pâté and a mousse. A pâté usually contains quite a lot of butter, but as this recipe uses none, it will be light and fluffy. The pâté cries out for soda bread. If you prefer, you can make your own but I find my method just a weenie bit quicker!!

Put ¼ of a lemon, skin, pith etc., into a food processor and blend. Add smoked trout, cream cheese, dill (reserve a few sprigs for decoration), pepper and blend until smooth. Put into a serving bowl or 8 ramekin dishes and chill for at least 1 hour.

◑ May be made the day before.

✳ May be frozen.

To heat soda bread – sprinkle water over the bread to dampen and wrap in silver foil. Put in oven: 190°C, 375°F, Gas Mark 5 for 10 minutes. Slice the remaining lemons and serve pâté with a sprig of dill, lemon slice and warm soda bread.

Opposite: Sicilian Nights (page 42)

BEEF, WILD MUSHROOM AND SMOKED OYSTERS IN GUINNESS WITH PUFF PASTRY SHAMROCKS

500g (1lb 2oz) shallots – peeled (see Cook's tips)
1 tbsp olive oil
1 oz butter
2 tbsp brown sugar
1.25kg (2lbs 12oz) sirloin steak – trim off any fat and cut into strips
2 packets mushroom soup e.g. Knorr
300ml (½pt) Guinness
600ml (1pt) water
250g (9oz) wild mushrooms – depending on size, sliced, cut in half or leave whole
2 tins (100g each) smoked oysters – drained
2 handfuls fresh chopped parsley
salt and pepper
1 packet (375g) ready rolled puff pastry for shamrocks – optional (see Cook's tips)
Oven: 190°C, 375°F, Gas Mark 5

 You can't have a St. Patrick's menu without Guinness, but if you don't want to drink it, cook with it instead (or do both). It gives this casserole a wonderfully rich and full flavour.

Heat the oil and butter in a large saucepan. Add shallots and sauté for 10 minutes with the lid on. Add sugar and beef and continue to cook for a couple more minutes to brown the meat. Add mushroom soup, Guinness, water and bring up to the boil. Simmer for 10 minutes, then add mushrooms and smoked oysters for another 10 minutes. Season and serve with chopped parsley and shamrocks.

◗ May be made the day before.

✳ May be frozen.

To re-heat – put in an oven- proof serving dish, cover and put in oven for 45 minutes – 1 hour or until piping hot.

To make the shamrocks – unroll the pastry and cut into shamrock shapes. Put on a baking tray in oven for 10 minutes and serve with the beef.

Cook's tips: To make the shallots easier to peel, put them in a bowl and pour boiling water over them. Leave them to stand for 10 minutes before peeling.
If you are going to make the pastry shamrocks, you will need a shamrock pastry cutter – available from specialist cake making shops or Ireland!

IRISH POTATO CAKE

Oil or butter for greasing
1.5kg (3lbs 5oz) potatoes – scrubbed
8 spring onions – chopped
200ml (7fl oz) milk
40g (1½oz) butter
1 tsp freshly ground nutmeg
2 tbsp Parmesan
salt and pepper

Like Guinness, you can't have an Irish menu without potatoes!

You will need a greased spring-form or loose-bottomed cake tin – approx 24cm (9½"). Cut the potatoes into chunks, boil until soft and drain well. Melt butter in the saucepan, add chopped spring onions and fry for 2 minutes. Return potatoes to the pan with milk, butter, nutmeg and season generously. Mash together and turn out into cake tin. Sprinkle Parmesan on top. If serving immediately, put under grill to brown for 5 minutes.

To serve – slide a knife around and remove the side of the tin. Leave cake on the base and place on a large serving plate. Cut into slices as you would a cake.

✳ May be made earlier in the day.

If making earlier, do not grill but put in oven: 220°C, 425°F, Gas Mark 7 to heat through for 40 minutes.

Cook's tip: This potato recipe may also be served just as "mash" without forming into a cake.

ROAST ROOT VEGETABLES WITH THYME

1 swede – peeled and cut into chunks

4 large parsnips – scrubbed and thickly sliced

6 large carrots – scrubbed and thickly sliced

2 onions – peeled and cut into eighths

2 handfuls fresh thyme

4 tbsp olive oil

salt and pepper

Oven: 220°C, 425°F, Gas Mark 7

I asked all my Irish friends which vegetables were traditionally eaten in Ireland and they all said "potato". But as I already had potato cake, I decided to use some root vegetables.

Put all ingredients in a large roasting tin and cook for 1 hour tossing half way through.

IRISH COFFEE PUDDING

150ml (¼pt) strong black coffee

200g (7oz) dark chocolate

425ml (¾pt) double cream

4 tbsp whisky and more!

1 packet (200g) bourbon biscuits – crushed

You only need a small amount of this mousse-type dessert as it is very rich. I like to serve it in little coffee cups or glasses to look like a real Irish coffee. I have done this and told my guests that, unfortunately, the pudding went wrong so I was serving coffee straight away. They got a pleasant surprise when they realised they were eating the most mind-blowing velvety, chocolatey dessert and that it was only one of my little jokes!

Melt chocolate with the coffee in a bowl over simmering water or in a microwave on medium for 3 minutes. Add 4 tbsp whisky to 300ml (½pt) of the cream and whisk until thick. Fold in melted chocolate and crushed bourbon biscuits. Put into small coffee cups or glasses, leaving enough room at the top for some more cream to be added, and chill for at least 1 hour.

◗ May be made up to this point the day before.

✳ May be frozen.

To serve   mix remaining cream with more whisky if required, and pour on top of mousses.

ORDER OF PREPARATION IF MAKING IN ADVANCE:

The day before:
1. Make the smoked trout pâté.
2. Make the beef recipe and cut out the shamrocks.
3. Make the Irish coffee pudding up to ◗

Earlier on the day:
4. Make the potato cake.

In the evening:
5. Prepare and cook the roast vegetables.
6. Re-heat the beef and cook shamrock as needed.
7. Re-heat potato cake.
8. Put soda bread in oven.
9. Pour cream over puddings just before serving.

ORDER OF PREPARATION IN UNDER 90 MINUTES:

1. Make trout pâté and heat bread as necessary.
2. Prepare roast vegetables and put in oven as needed.
3. Make Irish coffee pudding.
4. Make potato cake.
5. Make beef recipe.

SIMPLY RED

I used this menu for a party I had recently for 70 people. It had a theme where all the guests wore red, "Simply Red" music was playing throughout the evening and, of course, all the food was red. We decorated the house with red balloons and red crêpe paper, had red "pick 'n mix" sweets scattered around and bowls of mini Edam. I have made the quantities for 8 but you can multiply them if necessary. I decided to give the food a Moroccan touch which everyone agreed was very Moorish!

SPICY SALSA AND RED LEICESTER MINI TARTS

250g (9oz) ready-made short crust pastry

1 jar or tub (approx 200g) spicy tomato salsa

115g (4oz) red Leicester – grated

Oven: 190°C, 375°F, Gas Mark 5

These mini tarts are ideal for a party as they can be prepared in advance and they can be eaten with fingers, saving extra plates and washing up.

Roll out pastry thinly on a lightly floured work surface. Using a round pastry cutter (approx 6cm/2½" in diameter), cut out as many circles as you can – around 20-24. Put in tart or muffin sheets (if you only have one 12 holed sheet you will have to make them in two batches) and prick the bottoms with a fork. Put in oven for 10 minutes. Put a teaspoon of salsa in each tart and sprinkle the cheese on top.

◗ May be made up to this stage the day before.

Put back in oven for 10-15 minutes until cheese is bubbling. Serve warm.

Cook's tip: There are many different types of ready-made salsa around. I would recommend buying a mild one for those guests who don't like spicy things.

RED COUSCOUS

400g (14oz) couscous

1 tin (400g) chopped tomatoes

425ml (¾pt) vegetable, lamb or chicken stock – made with 1 stock cube and boiling water

salt and pepper

Traditionally couscous is served with tagines as the grains soak up all the delicious spiced juices.

Mix all ingredients together and leave to soak for 10 minutes.

☀ May be prepared earlier in the day.

Put in microwave on high for 5 minutes and fork through to break up any lumps.

Cook's tip: Put the couscous in a microwavable serving bowl so that it can be served straight from the microwave.

LAMB TAGINE WITH APRICOTS AND RED KIDNEY BEANS

3 tbsp olive oil

1kg (2lbs 4oz) cubed leg or shoulder of lamb – (see Cook's tip below)

2 red onions – thinly sliced

1 red pepper – de-seeded and sliced

3 tsp each of ground ginger, cinnamon, coriander, turmeric and cumin

2 tbsp plain flour

1litre (1¾pt) lamb or vegetable stock – made with 2 stock cubes and boiling water

250g (9oz) dried apricots

2 tins (400g each) red kidney beans – drained

salt and pepper

Tagine comes from Morocco and is the name given to the style of cooking as well the pot that it is cooked in. Traditionally this dish is cooked slowly in a large flame-proof pot with a round base and a high conical lid, for at least 2 hours after marinating for 2 hours. As this is "Dinners in a Dash" and speed is of the essence, I have used an alternative method which is far quicker.

Heat the olive oil in a large saucepan and add the lamb, sliced onions, red pepper, spices and flour. Fry for 5 minutes to allow meat and onions to brown. Add stock, bring up to the boil and simmer for 20 minutes. Add apricots and red kidney beans and simmer for a further 10 minutes.

◗ May be made the day before.

❄ May be frozen.

To re-heat – either return to saucepan and heat gently until piping hot or put in an oven-proof serving dish and cover with lid or foil. Put in oven: 190°C, 375°F, Gas Mark 5 for 45 minutes – 1 hour or until piping hot.

Cook's tip: Some supermarkets sell ready cubed leg of lamb which saves you having to do it yourself. If you cannot find this, try to get the leg or shoulder boned to make it easier to cut up and remove as much excess fat as possible.

BEETROOT, TOMATO AND RED ONION SALAD

500g (1lb 2oz) natural cooked beetroot – cut into cubes

8 medium sized tomatoes – cut into cubes

1 red onion – chopped

2 tsp cumin seeds

6 tbsp French dressing

salt and pepper

Carrying on the red theme, this salad produces a combination of the most beautiful shades of red.

Mix all ingredients together in a large salad bowl.

❄ May be prepared earlier in the day.

SUMMER FRUIT AND MASCARPONE CHEESECAKE WITH A RED FRUIT COULIS

❧ A friend who tested this cheesecake described it as being "better than sex" – try it and see.

300g (10½oz) rustic biscuits – "Hob Nobs" recommended

100g (3½oz) butter

250g (9oz) mascarpone

250g (9oz) fromage frais

4 tbsp castor sugar

4 eggs

500g (1lb 2oz) frozen summer fruit – defrosted

250g (9oz) frozen raspberries

1 tbsp icing sugar

Oven: 170°C, 325°F, Gas Mark 3

Grease a round spring-form or loose-bottomed cake tin – about 24cm (9 ½") in diameter. Roughly crush biscuits, melt butter, mix together and press into the base of the tin. Put in the fridge while you make the filling.

Beat or whisk mascarpone with fromage frais, sugar and eggs. Drain the summer fruit and reserve the juice for the coulis. Fold fruit into mascarpone mixture and pour into cake tin. Put the cake tin on a baking tray and put in oven for 1 hour. Turn the oven off but leave the cheesecake in oven for a further 15 minutes (this should help to prevent cracks forming). If you are in a hurry, just take the cheesecake out of the oven – the odd crack won't matter. To make coulis - put frozen raspberries in a food processor or liquidizer with juice from summer fruit and icing sugar.

◑ May be made the day before.

❅ The cheesecake may be frozen.

To serve – slide a flat knife round the edge of the tin and remove the sides. Keep the cheesecake on the base of the tin and put on a serving plate. Slice and serve with the coulis.

Cook's tip: If you are planning on freezing the cheesecake, it can be removed from the base of the tin while frozen. Slide a palate knife between the base of the cheesecake and the tin and separate. Place on the plate on which you are going to serve it.

ORDER OF PREPARATION IF MAKING IN ADVANCE:

The day before:
1. Make cheesecake up to ◑
2. Make lamb tagine.
3. Make mini tarts.

Earlier on the day:
4. Make beetroot salad.
5. Prepare couscous up to ❅

In the evening:
5. Re-heat lamb and tarts.
6. Put couscous in microwave.

ORDER OF PREPARATION IN UNDER 90 MINUTES:

1. Make cheesecake and coulis (don't worry if it's still warm when you come to serve it as it will still taste great).
2. Make lamb tagine.
3. Prepare mini tarts and put in oven as needed.
4. Prepare couscous and put in microwave as needed.
5. Make beetroot salad.

SHORT CUT CASSOULET

♀ *A ripe New World Chardonnay.
Recommendation – Conch y Toro
Casillero del Diablo Chardonnay
from Chile.*

*T*his menu is a real example of fusion cooking, bringing together
ingredients from different countries to form some really
original dishes.*

CHORIZO, COUSCOUS AND PINE NUT SALAD

Chorizo is a spicy Spanish sausage made out of pork and paprika. It can be quite chewy (my daughter adores it and calls it "string") and compliments the fluffy couscous and crunch of the pine nuts.

Mix together couscous, orange juice, sliced chorizo, pine nuts, salt and pepper. Leave to soak for 20 minutes or overnight.

◑ May be prepared up to this stage the day before.

Arrange leaves on individual plates. Mix couscous with a fork to break up any lumps and place on top of leaves. Drizzle over olive oil and decorate with orange slices.

Cook's tip: Peppery flavoured salad leaves such as watercress or rocket go especially well with this starter.

175g (6oz) couscous
300ml (½pt) orange juice
1 chorizo sausage (approx 225g (8oz) – outer skin removed and thinly sliced
100g (3½oz) pine nuts
200g mixed salad leaves
4 tbsp olive oil
2 oranges – sliced
salt and pepper

CASSOULET OF SEAFOOD WITH FLAGEOLET AND FENNEL

Cassoulet is traditionally made with pork and haricot beans. This is a fishy variation with flageolet beans and fennel all cooked together in the same pot to create wonderful flavours. It is a cross between a stew and a soup and can be served on a plate or in large soup bowls.

Scrub mussels and keep in a bowl of salted water. Put all other ingredients into a large casserole dish and mix together.

☼ May be prepared up to this stage earlier in the day.

Drain mussels and add to casserole. Cover and cook in oven for 45 minutes – 1 hour until cooked through and piping hot. Sprinkle chopped fennel feathers on top and serve with ciabatta croutons.

Cook's tip: There are some excellent fish soups around. The ones in jars are better than the tinned variety and I recommend "Select Marée" or Waitrose own brand. Mussels should be bought on the day on which they are going to be eaten. They should be tightly closed before cooking and open when cooked. Discard any that don't open once cooked.

450g (1lb) fresh mussels in shells – (see Cook's tip below)
450g (1lb) white fish, e.g. cod or haddock, skinned and cut in chunks
225g (8oz) prawns – uncooked and shelled
1 dressed crab or 1 tin crab meat
2 tins (400g each) flageolet beans – drained
2 fennel bulbs – sliced (reserve the feathered leaves for decoration and chop)
2 garlic cloves – crushed
1 jar (approx 800ml) fish soup
salt and pepper
Oven: 190°C, 375°F, Gas Mark 5

GRUYÈRE CIABATTA CROUTONS

1 ciabatta

1 clove garlic

150g (5oz) Gruyère – grated

Oven: 190°C, 375°F, Gas Mark 5

These croutons are great to mop up all the "gravy" from the cassoulet. Cut ciabatta into 16 slices and grill until golden. Rub garlic clove on to one side of each slice and place on a baking tray.

☼ May be prepared to this stage earlier in the day.

Sprinkle grated Gruyère on top and put in oven for 10 minutes or under a pre-heated grill until cheese has melted.

BRAISED GLAZED CHICORY

8 heads of chicory – halved lengthways

40g (1½oz) butter or "Olivio"

1 tbsp brown sugar

2 tbsp white wine

salt and pepper

Oven: 190°C, 375°F, Gas Mark 5

Chicory is delicious cooked but tends to be slightly bitter. The sugar counters the bitterness and gives a lovely glazed effect.

Spread the butter over the base of an oven-proof serving or gratin dish. Sprinkle over sugar and add wine. Arrange chicory in dish, cut side down, in a single layer and season. Cover with foil.

☼ May be prepared up to this point earlier in the day.

Cook in oven for 30 minutes and serve.

INDIVIDUAL TARTE TATIN WITH A MAPLE WALNUT SAUCE

4 medium apples

150ml (¼pt) maple syrup

25g (1oz) butter

100g (3½oz) walnut pieces

1 packet (375g) ready-rolled puff pastry

300ml (½pt) double cream

Oven: 200°C, 400°F, Gas Mark 6

Making a Tarte Tatin can be quite tricky. First of all you need a frying pan that can go in the oven which so many people don't possess. Secondly, the tarte is cooked upside down and turning it out can end up with a rather sticky mess. In this recipe you will need a bun sheet or 12 holed muffin tin. As they are made individually, they are easy to turn out using a spoon and palate knife, leaving a beautiful tarte on the plate.

There is no need to peel the apples. Remove core of apples with an apple corer and cut in half horizontally. Heat the butter with 3 tbsp of the maple syrup in a large frying pan, add apples and cook gently on both sides for about 5 minutes.

Put apples in a 12 hole bun sheet (rounded side down) with any "gunge" from the pan. Stuff half the walnuts inside the apples and allow to cool. Cut the pastry with a pastry cutter into 8 rounds (approx. 8cm/3¼" in diameter) and put on top of apples, tucking the sides down around the apples. Mix remaining walnuts with remaining maple syrup and cream.

◖ May be prepared up to this point the day before.

Put tartes in oven for 30 minutes. Heat the sauce in a saucepan until warm through.

Turn the Tarte Tatins out of the tins and serve with the sauce.

Cook's tip: The sauce may be served cold if preferred.

Opposite: Oriental Buffet (page 51)

ORDER OF PREPARATION IF MAKING IN ADVANCE:

The day before:
1. Make chorizo salad up to ◑
2. Make Tarte Tatin up to ◑

Earlier on the day:
3. Prepare cassoulet up to ☀
4. Prepare ciabatta croutons up to ☀
5. Prepare chicory up to ☀

In the evening:
6. Add mussels to cassoulet and put in oven as necessary.
7. Put chicory in oven.
8. Finish off chorizo salad.
9. Heat ciabatta croutons.
10. Put Tarte Tatins in oven while eating main course and heat sauce.

ORDER OF PREPARATION IN UNDER 90 MINUTES:

1. Prepare chorizo salad and place on individual plates before serving.
2. Prepare cassoulet and put in oven as needed.
3. Prepare Tarte Tatins and keep in fridge until ready to cook.
4. Prepare chicory and put in oven as needed.
5. Make ciabatta croutons and put in oven as needed.

Opposite: Mackerel On The Barbecue (page 57)

SICILIAN NIGHTS

♀ *A crisp, fresh Italian white.*
Recommendation – Frascati, Coli de
Catone from Italy

"*E il sesto giorno, Iddio, compi il suo lavoro e lieto d'aver creato tanto bello, Prese la terra tra le mani e la bacio. La, la dove lui poso le labra, e la Sicilia*"

"*And on the 6th day, God, having completed his task and being satisfied of such a beautiful creation, took the earth in his hands and kissed it. There, precisely where his lips touched it, is Sicily*".

RENZO BARBERA

Such a stunningly beautiful island needs a stunningly beautiful menu to go with it.

BRESAOLA WITH ARTICHOKES AND PARMESAN SHAVINGS SERVED WITH GARLIC AND BASIL PIZZA

32 slices bresaola
1 tin (400g) artichoke hearts – drained and cut into quarters
100g (3½oz) Parmesan
4 tbsp olive oil
1 tbsp balsamic vinegar
GARLIC AND BASIL PIZZA
4 medium or 2 large pizza bases
olive oil
4 garlic cloves – chopped or crushed
2 handfuls torn basil leaves
salt and pepper
Oven: 190°C, 375°F, Gas Mark 5

Bresaola is air-dried beef which is then matured for several months. It is a speciality from Lombardy in Italy and is an ideal base for this quite delicious light starter.

To make garlic and basil pizzas – brush pizza bases with olive oil, sprinkle garlic and basil on top and season. Put straight on to the rack/shelf in oven for 10 minutes. Cut into wedges and serve.

Put 4 slices bresaola on each plate and place artichoke quarters on top. Make Parmesan shavings with a potato peeler and sprinkle on top. Drizzle with olive oil and balsamic vinegar.

Cook's tips: If you have problems finding bresaola, use parma ham or proscuitto instead. Pizza bases are available from most supermarkets.

SALMON AND ASPARAGUS ON A BED OF RICOTTA-FILLED RAVIOLI

There are many different types of ready-made fresh ravioli. The type filled with ricotta go best with this recipe and they may also have the addition of something like broccoli, spinach or asparagus.

Use a shallow non-metallic oven-proof dish for this recipe. Mix together crème fraîche, soup, wine or vermouth, garlic and season. Cut any woody ends off the asparagus and cut asparagus spears in half. Cut salmon into 2.5cm (1") chunks and add to crème fraîche mixture with asparagus. Cover with foil.

◐ May be prepared up to this stage the day before.

Cook in oven for 30 minutes. Cook ravioli according to instructions on packet. Serve ravioli with salmon mixture on top.

Cook's tip: An easy way to cook pasta so that you don't have to watch over it as it cooks is to bring water up to boil in a large saucepan with salt and 1 tbsp oil. Plunge ravioli in, leave to boil for a minute, then turn off heat, cover pan with a lid and leave to stand for up to half an hour. Drain and serve.

1 tub (200ml) crème fraîche (the half fat type may be used)

1 tin "Campbell's Condensed Cream of Asparagus" Soup

1 glass white wine or dry vermouth

2 garlic cloves – crushed

200g (7oz) baby asparagus

900g (2lbs) salmon fillets – skinned

1kg (2lbs 4oz) ready-made ricotta-filled ravioli

salt and pepper

Oven: 190°C, 375°F, Gas Mark 5

CARAMELISED RED ONION AND BLUEBERRY SALAD

Thanks go to my friend Rebecca for yet another idea for a recipe. This combination of ingredients makes a deliciously unusual salad. Watch the surprise on your guests' faces when they bite into the blueberries thinking they're black olives!

Heat the oil in a frying pan. Add sliced onions and brown sugar and cook over a medium heat for 10 minutes until onions have become brown, sticky and caramelised. Leave to cool.

◐ May be prepared up to this point the day before.

Put salad leaves into a large salad bowl and toss together with caramelised onions, blueberries, dressing, salt and pepper

Cook's tip: If blueberries are not available, use other fruit like small seedless grapes, raspberries or just leave the fruit out altogether.

2 tbsp olive oil

2 red onions – sliced

2 heaped tbsp brown sugar

400g mixed salad leaves

250g (9oz) blueberries

6 tbsp ready-made dressing

salt and pepper

ICED TIRAMISU TERRINE WITH A MARSALA SAUCE

1.5 litres coffee ice cream

1 packet (200g) Boudoirs Biscuits (Ladies Fingers)

Marsala (Madeira or sweet sherry may be used instead)

1 tub (400ml) ready-made custard (preferably fresh)

100g (3½oz) dark chocolate – grated

Marsala is a sweet dessert wine made from grapes grown in the western part of Sicily. It is traditionally used when making tiramisu which has become increasing popular in the U.K. I have come up with a variation – an iced tiramisu terrine. It makes a change and looks very pretty when sliced and served with the Marsala sauce.

Allow ice cream to soften slightly. Line a 1.5 litre terrine tin with foil. Spread ⅓ of the ice cream in the bottom of the tin. Lay half the biscuits on top in a single layer and drizzle over 3 tbsp of Marsala. Repeat with another ⅓ of ice cream, the remaining biscuits, drizzle with Marsala and top with the remaining ice cream. Put in freezer for at least 90 minutes.

To make the sauce – mix custard with 4-6 tbsp Marsala.

◑ The sauce may be made the day before.

✳ The iced terrine may be kept in the freezer for up to two months.

To serve – turn terrine out onto a serving plate and remove foil. Slice, serve with sauce and sprinkle grated chocolate on top.

Cook's tip: This recipe can also be made using chocolate ice cream.

ORDER OF PREPARATION IF MAKING IN ADVANCE:

The day before:
1. Make salmon recipe up to ◑
2. Make salad up to ◑
3. Make tiramisu and sauce ◑

In the evening:
4. Make starter and put pizzas in oven as needed.
5. Put salmon in oven and cook ravioli as needed.
6. Finish off salad.
7. Turn tiramisu out onto a serving plate.

ORDER OF PREPARATION IN UNDER 90 MINUTES:

1. Make tiramisu and sauce.
2. Prepare salad up to ◑ and toss in other ingredients just before serving.
3. Prepare and cook salmon and asparagus mixture.
4. Make starter.
5. Cook ravioli.

BORDERING ON THE SWISS

*T*hese recipes are a real mixture of French, Italian and German cuisine therefore perfect for this menu. I have had many skiing holidays around this area and the following menu is a collection of all my favourite recipes.

FOCACCIA WITH MARINATED PEPPERS, OLIVES AND ANCHOVIES

2 large focaccia
2 garlic cloves
2 jars (280g each) peppers in oil or tomato dressing
1 small tin pitted black olives – drained and cut in half
1 tin anchovies – drained
60g (2oz) rocket leaves

Focaccia is an Italian flat bread made with olive oil. Nowadays, it is readily available from most large supermarkets and comes with many different toppings, such as herbs, sun-dried tomatoes and other varieties. This recipe can either be served as a starter on individual plates, or passed around on a large platter for people to eat in their fingers with drinks.

Cut focaccia into 1.5cm (½") slices. Grill on both sides until golden. Peel garlic cloves and rub garlic on to one side of the toasted focaccia. Brush the same side with oil (taken from the jars of peppers if possible), top with drained peppers, olives and anchovies. Cut slices in half and either arrange on a large platter or on individual plates with the rocket leaves.

Cook's tip: There are many variations to this recipe with many different toppings, for example, marinated jars of artichoke hearts or mushrooms topped with capers, goats cheese, mozzarella, etc.

BOURSIN STUFFED CHICKEN BREASTS WRAPPED IN PANCETTA

8 skinless chicken breasts
150g (5oz) garlic Boursin
8 slices pancetta
2 glasses dry white wine
100g (3½oz) fromage frais
salt and pepper
Oven: 190°C, 375°F, Gas Mark 5

This recipe is made wonderfully garlicky by the Boursin. If you prefer, you can use a soft cream cheese with crushed garlic added. Pancetta is Italian streaky bacon and is used to flavour many dishes.

Cut slits in the chicken breasts lengthways and open out like a book. Use half the Boursin to spread inside the breasts, season with pepper and fold up. Wrap each breast in a slice of pancetta and put in an oven proof serving dish or baking dish with the fold at the bottom.

To make the sauce – mix remaining Boursin with wine and season.

◑ May be prepared up to this stage the day before.

Cook chicken, uncovered, in oven for 35 minutes. Gently heat the Boursin and wine mixture in a saucepan to make the sauce. When the chicken is cooked, add the juices from the pan to the sauce. Take the sauce off the heat and stir in the fromage frais. Serve sauce with chicken.

Cook's tip: Don't worry if the Boursin oozes out of the chicken a bit – it will add extra flavour to the sauce.

POTATO AND COURGETTE RÖSTI

Why take hours making your own rösti when you can buy it in packets? And even better still, mix it with some courgettes to add a bit of colour and flavour and fool your guests that you must have made it yourself.

Grease one large or two medium sized oven-proof serving or gratin dishes. Put the rösti in a large bowl and break up with a fork. Grate the courgettes (may be done in a food processor) and mix with rösti and season. Put into oven dish.

◗ May be prepared up to this stage the day before.

Put in oven for 1 hour.

4 medium courgettes

3 packets rösti

salt and pepper

Oven: 200ºC, 400ºF, Gas Mark 6

SUGAR SNAP PEAS IN LEMON BUTTER

Lovely sweet, crisp sugar snap peas are cooked briefly to preserve their crispness and simply tossed in lemon butter.

Plunge sugar snap peas into boiling water for 5 minutes. Drain and toss in remaining ingredients.

Cook's tip: You can buy ready topped and tailed sugar snap peas if you're in a real hurry.

800g (1lb 12oz) sugar snap peas – top and tail

zest and juice ½ lemon

25g (1oz) butter or "Olivio"

salt and pepper

MOCHA TARTE WITH GRAND MARNIER CREAM

If you like to finish a meal with chocolate followed by coffee and liqueurs, then this pudding is ideal as it includes all three.

Roll out pastry and line a tart tin (preferably loose-bottomed) 28cm (11") in diameter. Prick the base with a fork and put in fridge while preparing the filling.

Melt the chocolate, black coffee and cream in a saucepan over a gentle heat until chocolate has dissolved (do not allow to boil). Take off the heat and beat in the eggs. Pour into the prepared pastry case and cook in oven for 50 minutes.

To make the Grand Marnier cream – add the Grand Marnier and icing sugar to the cream and whisk until stiff.

◗ May be prepared up to this point the day before.

250g (9oz) ready-made short crust pastry

200g (7oz) dark chocolate

150ml (¼pt) very strong black coffee

300ml (½pt) double cream

3 eggs

1 tbsp icing sugar

GRAND MARNIER CREAM

300ml (½pt) whipping or double cream

large slug (approx 4 tbsp) Grand Marnier

1 tbsp icing sugar

Oven: 180ºC, 350ºF, Gas Mark 4

✳ May be frozen.

To re-heat the tart – put in oven for 15 minutes, sieve icing sugar over the top and serve with Grand Marnier cream.

Cook's tip: I prefer to serve the tart hot, but it can also be eaten cold or at room temperature.

ORDER OF PREPARATION IF MAKING IN ADVANCE:

The day before:
1. Make Boursin chicken up to ◖
2. Make rösti up to ◖
3. Make mocha tarte and Grand Marnier cream.

In the evening:
4. Make starter.
5. Prepare sugar snap peas and cook as needed.
6. Cook chicken and heat sauce.
7. Put rösti in oven as needed.

ORDER OF PREPARATION IN UNDER 90 MINUTES:

1. Prepare chicken and sauce and cook as necessary.
2. Prepare and cook rösti.
3. Prepare sugar snap peas.
4. Make tarte but don't put in oven until 50 minutes before you are going to need it.
5. Make starter.

ALFRESCO

♀ *A crisp, fresh Italian white.*
Recommendation – Feudi di San
Gregorio Falanghina from Italy

*T*here's no doubt that food tastes wonderful eaten in the fresh air, on a warm balmy day, under a cloudless blue sky with a beautiful view. This menu can be eaten anywhere – it's easily transportable for an elegant picnic by a lake, river or even the back garden (or kitchen if it rains).

FOCACCIA WITH MASCARPONE AND SWEET ONION COMPOTE

3 tbsp olive oil
4 large onions – thinly sliced
4 tbsp brown sugar
4 tbsp balsamic vinegar
salt and pepper
2 loaves focaccia
250g (9oz) mascarpone

Focaccia is a round Italian bread made with olive oil. It is available from most supermarkets with different toppings, such as herb, sun-dried tomato. Buy which ever one you like as any of them will go well with the mascarpone and the lovely sweet caramelised onion compote.

Heat the oil in a large saucepan, add onions and brown sugar, cover and fry for about 5 minutes to brown. Turn the heat down, and continue to cook gently for a further 10 minutes to soften. Take off heat and add balsamic vinegar. Leave to cool.

◗ The sweet onion compote may be made the day before.

Cut focaccia in half horizontally and grill each side for 1-2 minutes until golden. Spread each side with mascarpone and season. Spread onion compote on top.

☀ May be prepared up to this stage earlier in the day.

To serve – slice into wedges.

Cook's tip: This may also be served warm by putting in oven: 190°C, 375°F, Gas Mark 5 for 10 minutes.

TAPENADE STUFFED SALMON WITH MARINATED MEDITERRANEAN VEGETABLES

1 whole salmon (approx weight 2.25kg/5lbs) ask supermarket or fishmonger to skin and fillet it – alternatively buy 2 whole salmon fillets (approx total weight 1.3kg/3lbs)

½ jar (80g) green olive tapenade

3½ lemons

1 jar (190g) marinated vegetables, e.g. "Sacla" Olive and Tomato Pastagusto

1 tub (200ml) crème fraîche – the half fat type may be used

bunch watercress

350g (12oz) black olives

salt and pepper

Oven: 190°C, 375°F, Gas Mark 5

This is a lovely "Summery" way of cooking salmon and can be eaten hot or cold. The salmon is stuffed with an olive paste and even if you don't usually like olives, you'll love them in this form. It's also an ideal recipe for entertaining large numbers for a buffet as it can all be prepared in advance, looks colourful and very impressive.

Spread the olive tapenade inside the salmon fillets, season and pour over the juice of ½ lemon. Wrap tightly in foil. Cook in oven for 30 minutes and leave to cool in the foil.

Mix marinated vegetables with the crème fraîche and the juice of 1 lemon. Put into a serving bowl and serve with salmon.

◖ May be prepared up to this stage the day before.

To serve – unwrap salmon and discard the juices. Place on a large serving platter. Cut the remaining 2 lemons into wedges and put around the edge of the salmon together with the watercress and black olives. Serve with marinated vegetables.

Cook's tips: If you don't have a large enough serving platter, slice the salmon and arrange the slices with other ingredients as above. If you are going to serve the salmon hot, then cook it for a total of 45 minutes.

ROAST TOMATO AND BASIL SALAD

16 medium tomatoes

2 garlic cloves – chopped

1 tsp sugar

3 handfuls basil

4 tbsp olive oil

2 tbsp balsamic vinegar

salt and pepper

Oven: 190°C, 375°F, Gas Mark 5

A marriage made in heaven (apart from mine). How did we ever survive without tomatoes and basil?

Cut tomatoes in half through the equator and put in a roasting tin, cut sides up, in one layer. Sprinkle the garlic, sugar, half the basil chopped and season.

Pour olive oil on top and put in oven for 40 minutes.

Take out of oven and drizzle with balsamic vinegar while still hot. Leave to cool.

◖ May be made the day before.

Put onto a serving platter and decorate with remaining basil leaves before serving.

Cook's tip: As an alternative, these tomatoes may be served hot straight from the oven.

TORTELLINI AND ROCKET SALAD

Tortellini are small pasta circles with various fillings. They are usually filled with ricotta or other Italian cheese or possibly a vegetable such as spinach. They can be bought fresh or in long-life packets.

500g (1lb 2oz) fresh tortellini with the filling of your choice

8 tbsp Italian dressing – Waitrose recommended

salt and pepper

60g (2oz) rocket leaves

Cook tortellini as instructions on the packet. Drain and toss in dressing and season while still hot.

◑ May be prepared up to this stage the day before.

Toss together with rocket leaves just before serving.

SUMMER FRUIT TARTLETTES

This is a variation of a summer pudding made into individual tarts. Not only do they look pretty but are easy to eat alfresco.

8 slices white bread – thin or medium

oil, for brushing

150g (5oz) strawberries – sliced

100g (3½oz) raspberries

100g (3½oz) blueberries

3 tbsp strawberry or raspberry jam

3 tbsp kirsch or water

Oven: 190°C, 375°F, Gas Mark 5

Roll out bread with a rolling pin to make the slices slightly larger and thinner. With a round pastry cutter (approx. 6cm (2½") in diameter) cut two rounds out of each slice of bread. Push the 16 rounds into muffin or tart tins and lightly brush with oil (you may have to do this in 2 batches if you only have one 12 holed muffin tray). Put in oven for 12 minutes until golden. Leave to cool.

◑ May be prepared the day before.

Put the jam and kirsch or water in a saucepan and put over a gentle heat to dissolve. Mix with sliced strawberries, raspberries and blueberries to coat. Fill tart cases with fruit mixture.

☀ The tarts may be filled an hour or so before serving.

May be served on their own or with cream or ice cream.

Cook's tip: If you have an abundance of summer fruits growing in your garden, e.g. blackberries, they may be substituted for the fruits mentioned above.

ORDER OF PREPARATION IF MAKING IN ADVANCE:

The day before:
1. Make sweet onion compote.
2. Cook salmon and mix marinated vegetables.
3. Cook tomatoes.
4. Make tortellini salad up to ◑
5. Make tarts up to ◑

Earlier on the day:
6. Finish off focaccia recipe.
7. Fill tarts.

Before serving:
8. Toss rocket into tortellini.

ORDER OF PREPARATION IN UNDER 90 MINUTES (this will mean that the starter, salmon and salads will be served warm)

1. Make tart cases and prepare filling. Fill tarts before serving.
2. Cook salmon and mix marinated vegetables.
3. Cook tomatoes.
4. Make starter.
5. Make tortellini salad.

ORIENTAL BUFFET

♀ *A spicy white.*
Recommendation – Casablanca,
Gewürztraminer from Chile

*T*his menu will impress your friends on a warm summer's evening or even on a picnic, as it's easily transportable. It's ideal for large parties as you can increase the quantities and virtually everything can be prepared in advance.

ORIENTAL HORS D'OEUVRE WITH THAI DIPPING SAUCES

200g (7oz) squid rings

300g (10½oz) cooked, shelled prawns

200g (7oz) baby corn

200g (7oz) radishes

1 packet ready to eat poppadoms or mini poppadoms

dipping sauces (– see Cook's tip)

A lovely informal starter to get your friends chatting. The success of this starter is in the presentation and it looks great arranged on a very large platter. All the items I have suggested are served cold but if you want something hot, you can serve ready-made spring rolls, prawn toasts or other similar oriental finger food which most of the large supermarkets sell.

You will need to cook the squid first by dropping into boiling water for 2 minutes and then draining. Allow to cool.

✳ May be prepared earlier in the day.

Put dipping sauces into ramekin dishes. Arrange everything on a large platter for people to help themselves.

Cook's tip: There are many ready-made dipping sauces on the market. Blue Dragon do an excellent variety pack with chilli, hoi sin, satay and sweet and sour sauces.

THAI PRESIDENTIAL CHICKEN

8 chicken breasts – cooked and skinned (see Cook's tip below)

4 tsp Green Thai Curry Paste (Barts Spices recommended)

1 carton (200ml) coconut cream

8 heaped tbsp mayonnaise (approx 300ml)

2 heaped tbsp lime or lemon marmalade

3 handfuls chopped coriander

3 limes

1 large pawpaw

4 kiwi fruit

salt and pepper

You must be fed up with Coronation chicken by now, so I have come up with an Oriental version. As there is no King or Queen in Thailand, note the title!

Mix together curry paste, coconut cream, mayonnaise, marmalade, 2 handfuls of chopped coriander, zest and juice of 1 lime and season. Slice chicken and add to mixture.

◑ May be prepared up to this point the day before.

Peel the pawpaw, remove the seeds and slice. Peel and slice the kiwi fruit. Cut the remaining 2 limes into wedges. Put chicken on to a large serving platter, decorate with fruit and lime wedges and sprinkle remaining handful of chopped coriander on top.

Cooks' tip: To save time, I would recommend buying the chicken breasts ready cooked.

WILD RICE SALAD WITH BASIL AND SESAME OIL

400g (14oz) mixed long-grain and wild rice

3 tbsp fish sauce

3 tbsp sesame oil

salt and pepper

2 handfuls basil – shredded

You can buy packets of long-grain and wild rice ready mixed which gives a good texture and colour.

Cook rice as instructions on packet and drain. Mix with fish sauce, sesame oil, salt and pepper while hot. Allow to cool.

◗ May be prepared up to this point the day before.

Add shredded basil before serving.

BROCCOLI AND ALMOND SALAD WITH AN ORIENTAL DRESSING

500g (1lb 2oz) broccoli

1 Chinese cabbage

100g (3½oz) toasted flaked almonds

8 tbsp ready-made Thai or Oriental dressing – see Cook's tip below.

In this recipe not only are the broccoli florets used, but also the stalks. They are blanched for only a short time so that, together with the almonds and Chinese cabbage, they give this salad a real crunch.

Slice the stalks of the broccoli and break the heads up into florets. Blanch in boiling water for 3 minutes. Drain, rinse in cold water and put in a large salad bowl. Pour dressing over the broccoli.

☼ May be made up to this point earlier in the day.

Shred the Chinese cabbage and add to the broccoli together with the flaked almonds. Toss and serve.

Cook's tip: There are some ready-made oriental dressings around and some of the fresh stir-fry sauces also make good dressings.

LIME AND COCONUT CHEESECAKE

200g (7oz) gingernut biscuits – crushed

55g (2oz) butter - melted

1 packet (145g) lime jelly

1 tin (400ml) coconut milk

1 lime

450g (1lb) cream cheese – low fat or curd cheese may be used

100g (3½oz) desiccated coconut

2 star fruit

 A lovely refreshing cheesecake with all the flavours of the Orient.

You will need a spring-form cake tin about 24cm (9½") in diameter. Mix the crushed biscuits with the melted butter and push down into the tin. Put in fridge while making the filling.

Put jelly and ¼ of the coconut milk in a saucepan and heat gently until dissolved (or microwave on high for 2 minutes). Put into a mixing bowl and add remaining coconut milk, zest and juice of lime, desiccated coconut and cream cheese. Whisk together gently or beat with a spoon until smooth. Pour into cake tin and chill for at least 1½ to 2 hours.

◗ May be made the day before.

✳ May be frozen.

Slice the star fruit and use to decorate the cheesecake.

Cook's tip: To speed up the chilling process, put the cheesecake in the freezer for 20 minutes then transfer to the fridge.

ORDER OF PREPARATION IF MAKING IN ADVANCE:

The day before:
1. Make cheesecake.
2. Make Presidential chicken.
3. Make rice salad.

Earlier on the day:
4. Cook the squid.
5. Make broccoli salad up to ☀

In the evening:
1. Arrange hors d'oeuvre and sauces.
2. Finish off salad.

ORDER OF PREPARATION IN UNDER 90 MINUTES.

1. Make cheesecake and put in freezer for 20 minutes before transferring to fridge.
2. Cook squid, allow to cool before assembling hors d'oeuvres.
3. Make rice salad.
4. Cook broccoli, toss in dressing and add other ingredients before serving.
5. Make Thai chicken.

GRAB A CRAB

♀ *A ripe New World Chardonnay. Recommendation – Casablanca White Label Chardonnay from Chile*

*S*o many people are put off buying these ten-legged crustacea as they're not sure how to prepare and cook them. These days most supermarkets and fishmongers sell ready-dressed, cooked crab so all the work is done for you. They can be eaten cold straight from the shell or can be cooked. Crab is quite filling so I have allowed 6 crabs between 8 people making it a less extravagant meal than you might think.

GARLIC MUSHROOMS ON BRUSCHETTA

5 tbsp olive oil
4 cloves garlic – peeled and sliced
800g (1lb 12oz) large flat mushrooms – sliced
1 tub (200ml) crème fraîche – the half fat type may be used
1 glass white wine
3 handfuls chopped parsley
salt and pepper
1 ciabatta
Oven: 200°C, 400°F, Gas Mark 6

One of my favourite lunch-time restaurants in Tenerife called "Panchos", cooks wonderful garlic mushrooms where they are baked in olive oil with lots of whole garlic cloves. Being a lover of garlic, I eat the whole cloves (in fact I almost prefer them to the mushrooms!), so my dining companion did the same. He commented later in the day that he was amazed how well the mushrooms went with almonds! In this recipe, I have suggested slicing the garlic so that your friends aren't also mistaken.

Heat 2 tbsp olive oil in a large saucepan and add the sliced garlic. Fry for 2-3 minutes and add mushrooms, crème fraîche, wine and 2 handfuls parsley. Cook gently, stirring occasionally for a further 15 minutes. Season and serve with bruschetta or re-heat as below.

※ May be prepared up to this stage earlier in the day.

To make bruschetta – cut ciabatta into 16 slices, put on a baking tray and drizzle the remaining 3 tbsp olive oil on top. Put in oven for 5 minutes. Re-heat mushrooms in saucepan over a gentle heat for 10 minutes and serve with bruschetta. Sprinkle remaining parsley on top.

GRATIN OF CRAB AND ROCKET

6 large dressed crabs
50g (2oz) rocket leaves – shredded
1 tub (300-350g) ready-made cheese sauce
200g (7oz) Gruyère – grated
8 tbsp brown breadcrumbs – made from 2½ slices brown bread
2 lemons – cut into 8 wedges
salt and pepper
Oven: 200°C, 400°F, Gas Mark 6

This dish looks exceptionally impressive cooked in the shell of the crab. The recipe only calls for 6 crabs, so the first time you make it, you may have to serve it in gratin dishes (that's unless you happen to have a couple of spare crab shells knocking around). Reserve the shells to keep for the next time you are making this recipe.

Remove crab from shells and mix with ¾ of the shredded rocket, cheese sauce, half the cheese, salt and pepper. Put back into the shells, or into individual gratin dishes. Mix remaining cheese with breadcrumbs and sprinkle on top.

◗ May be prepared up to this stage the day before (assuming the crab is very fresh when you buy it).

Put in oven for 15 minutes. Serve with the remaining shredded rocket sprinkled on top and lemon wedges on the side.

Cook's tip: The best way to wash the shells is in a dish-washer. It gets them really clean and stops them smelling.

NEW POTATOES WITH RED PESTO

1.3kg (3lbs) new potatoes

½ jar (95g) red pesto

These lovely new potatoes, oozing with garlicky pesto, can be served hot or cold. I prefer them served hot with this menu, but if you prefer, you can cook them in advance, toss them in the pesto while hot and leave them to cool to serve as a potato salad.

Put potatoes into boiling water and simmer for 10 - 15 minutes. Drain, return to pan and toss together with pesto.

Cook's tip: I prefer to use red pesto as it gives a better colour but green pesto may also be used.

SPINACH, PANCETTA AND AVOCADO SALAD

80g (approx 8 slices) pancetta

2 avocados

2 bags (200g each) baby spinach leaves

8 tbsp ready-made French dressing

salt and pepper

Pancetta is an Italian streaky bacon with a wonderful depth of flavour. It is grilled or fried to add a lovely crispness to this salad. Bacon may be used instead of pancetta if you prefer.

Grill or fry the pancetta until crisp and golden and crumble into small pieces.

◗ May be prepared the day before.

Cut the avocados in half and remove the stones (see Cook's tip below). Scoop out the flesh with a teaspoon into bite-sized pieces. Toss all ingredients together.

Cook's tip: It is so difficult to buy avocados which are ripe at exactly the right moment. If they are too hard it is difficult to get the stone out but the easiest way to do so is to cut the avocado in half and separate the two halves. Stab a sharp knife in the stone and twist the knife. The stone should come out easily. If you prepare the avocado in advance, toss with lemon juice to prevent it discolouring.

ICED COFFEE MERINGUE CAKE WITH A MOCHA SAUCE

600ml (1pt) double or whipping cream

3 tbsp Camp coffee

large slug of brandy (approx 4 tbsp)

1 packet meringue nests (containing 6-8 meringues)

MOCHA SAUCE

4 heaped tbsp granulated sugar

200ml (7fl oz) water

3 heaped tbsp cocoa

3 tbsp Camp coffee

Due to the popularity of the "Iced Meringue Cake with a Raspberry Coulis" in my first book, I have been "bullied" into coming up with an alternative version for all those people who have made it so many times that they want a change. I have shocked myself by using "Camp Coffee" – not something I am particularly partial to, but it works brilliantly in this recipe.

Line a cake tin, 24cm (9½") in diameter, with cling-film. Whisk the cream, Camp coffee and brandy together until thick. Roughly crush the meringues and fold into the cream mixture. Put into the prepared cake tin and freeze for at least 2 hours.

To make mocha sauce – put the sugar and water into a saucepan and boil for 1 minute. Add cocoa, continue to boil while whisking until smooth. Take off the heat and add Camp coffee. The sauce should be quite runny and may be served hot or cold.

To serve – lift the iced meringue cake out of the tin, remove cling-film and put on a serving plate. Slice and serve with mocha sauce poured on top.

✳ The iced meringue cake may be stored in a freezer for up to 2 months.

◗ The mocha sauce may be stored in the fridge for up to a week.

Cook's tip: To save time, the iced meringue cake can be served with a bottle of ready-made chocolate sauce.

ORDER OF PREPARATION IF MAKING IN ADVANCE:

The day before:
1. Prepare the crab up to ◗
2. Cook the pancetta.
3. Make pudding.

Earlier on the day:
4. Make garlic mushrooms up to ✳

In the evening:
5. Prepare the bruschetta and put in oven as required.
6. Cook the potatoes and crab.
7. Make the salad.

ORDER OF PREPARATION IN UNDER 90 MINUTES:

1. Make pudding.
2. Prepare crab and cook as necessary.
3. Cook pancetta and toss with other salad ingredients just before serving.
4. Make garlic mushrooms and bruschetta.
5. Cook potatoes as required.

Opposite: 4TH July (page 60)

MACKEREL ON THE BARBECUE

♀ A crisp, herby Sauvignon Blanc.
Recommendation – Southern Right
Sauvignon Blanc from South Africa

*M*ost fish is delicious cooked on a barbecue and makes a change *from the usual chicken, ribs and sausages. I'm delighted that mackerel is gradually becoming more popular as it has so much going for it – it's cheap, extremely good for you and, if there are any, the left-overs taste great eaten cold.*

YELLOW SPLIT PEA, GARLIC AND BASIL PÂTÉ WITH BARBECUED BREAD

Don't be too shocked by the first ingredient – pease pudding! You're probably thinking of a stodgy "mush" piled beside the dried up Sunday roast. Well think again, because pease pudding is simply cooked and blended yellow split peas. Buying pease pudding means that you don't have any soaking or cooking – it's all done for you.

2 garlic cloves
3 handfuls basil
2 tins (420g) pease pudding
2 tbsp olive oil
1 tbsp balsamic vinegar
zest and juice of 1 lemon plus 2 lemons for decoration
salt and pepper
1 large "rustic type" loaf of bread or 2 medium loaves
250g (9oz) black olives (optional)

To make pâté – put garlic and 2 handfuls of the basil in a food processor to chop. Add all other ingredients except lemons for decoration, bread and olives and blend.

◖ May be prepared the day before.

✳ May be frozen.

Slice bread and toast on barbecue. Cut remaining lemons into wedges. Serve pâté with lemon wedges, black olives (optional) and barbecued bread.

Cook's tip: The pâté may be served in one large bowl or individual ramekin dishes. Alternatively, you can spread it on the toasted bread and hand it round on a large platter.

BARBECUED MACKEREL WITH GREMOLATA

Mackerel is the perfect fish to cook on a barbecue as it is naturally oily and therefore has a self-basting mechanism. Other types of fish may also be used in this recipe, e.g. trout, swordfish or monkfish. Gremolata comes from Italy and is made with garlic, parsley and lemon. My version is slightly different as I have added olive oil which makes it a perfect partner for the fish.

8 mackerel – gutted (heads may be removed if preferred)
GREMOLATA
4 handfuls parsley
3 garlic cloves
juice of 1 lemon
1 tsp sugar
8 tbsp olive oil
salt and pepper

Put all gremolata ingredients into a food processor to blend. Make 3 or 4 slits diagonally across the body of each mackerel on each side. Put in a non-metallic dish and using half the gremolata, rub all over the fish, inside and out. Leave to marinate for at least 30 minutes.

Opposite: Mystery Mustique (page 68)

◑ May be prepared the day before.

Cook on a hot barbecue or grill for about 6 minutes on each side, depending on the size of the fish. Serve with remaining gremolata.

Cook's tip: You will need a fish slice type utensil for turning the mackerel and don't worry if part of the skin gets stuck to the barbecue.

B.L.T. SALAD WITH A RANCH DRESSING

2 cos lettuce
8 medium tomatoes
250g (9oz) bacon – streaky or back
8 tbsp "Ranch Dressing"

As the famous B.L.T. (bacon, lettuce and tomato) sandwich has always been popular, I thought I'd turn it into a salad. I have suggested using "Ranch Dressing" – a creamy dressing very popular in America but it can also be served with French dressing if you prefer.

Shred lettuce, slice tomatoes and put into a large salad bowl. Cook the bacon on the barbecue until crisp (about 5 minutes). Chop bacon and toss together with lettuce, tomato and Ranch dressing.

Cook's tip: The bacon may be cooked in advance if you prefer.

NEW POTATO KEBABS

1.3kg (3lbs) new potatoes
olive oil – for brushing
salt and pepper

These potatoes can be prepared the day before and thrown on the barbecue to give them a delicious charred flavour. They are also very tasty with the gremolata.

Put potatoes into boiling water, simmer for 10 minutes and drain. Thread on to kebab sticks , brush with oil and season.

◑ May be prepared up to this stage the day before.

Cook on barbecue for about 5 minutes on each side.

Cook's tips: The quantity of potatoes given is quite generous. I would suggest making a few extra kebabs so you have seconds for hungry people. If you have a small barbecue and are worried about running out of room, barbecue the potatoes before the fish and keep warm or alternatively make a potato salad instead.

INDIVIDUAL ICED RHUBARB CRUMBLES

 Summer isn't summer without rhubarb but this recipe will save you the bother of preparing and cooking the rhubarb.

150ml (¼ pt) double cream
1 tub (400ml) fresh custard
1 jar (600g) rhubarb compote – "Bonne Maman" recommended
slug sweet sherry (approx 4 tbsp)
150g (5oz) digestive biscuits
8 tsp brown sugar

Whisk cream until thick and fold in custard, rhubarb and sherry. Put into 8 ramekin dishes. Crush digestive biscuits, sprinkle on top and finish off with the brown sugar. Put in freezer for at least 1 hour.

✳ May be kept in a freezer for up to 2 months.

Take out of freezer and put in fridge for 30 minutes before serving to allow crumbles to soften slightly.

Cook's tip: Other compotes may also be used, e.g. apricot or cherry.

ORDER OF PREPARATION IF MAKING IN ADVANCE:

The day before:
1. Make gremolata and marinate mackerel – there's no need to wash the food processor before making pâté.
2. Make pâté.
3. Prepare potato kebabs.
4. Make rhubarb crumble.

In the evening:
5. Prepare salad and cook bacon on barbecue as needed.
6. Toast bread on barbecue as needed.
7. Cook fish and potato kebabs.
8. Take rhubarb crumbles out of freezer.

ORDER OF PREPARATION IF MAKING IN UNDER 90 MINUTES:

1. Make rhubarb crumble.
2. Make gremolata (there's no need to wash processor before making pâté), marinate mackerel and put on barbecue as needed.
3. Make pâté and put bread on barbecue as necessary.
4. Prepare potatoes and barbecue when needed.
5. Prepare salad and cook bacon as needed.

4TH JULY

♀ *A full bodied, aromatic white. Fetzer Viognier from California*

*T*his is a lovely summer menu with an American theme – ideal for 4th July but tastes just as good on the 5th, 6th, 7th – or for any time of the year for that matter!

MINI CRISPY TARTS WITH PASTRAMI AND DILL CUCUMBER

❧ An ideal starter to eat with your fingers while having drinks, so that the cook/barbecuer is free to cook the tuna.

12 slices white bread
(thin or medium sliced)

olive oil

4 tsp grain mustard

4 heaped tbsp mayonnaise

1 pack (200g) wafer thin pastrami

1 jar (350g) sweet dill pickled cucumbers – sliced

Oven: 180°C, 350°F, Gas Mark 4

Roll slices of bread with a rolling pin to flatten. With a round pastry cutter (about 6cm/2½" in diameter) cut two rounds out of each slice of bread. Push the 24 rounds into tart or muffin tins and lightly brush with oil. Put in oven for 10 minutes until golden.

◗ May be made up to 2 days before and kept in an air-tight container.

Mix mustard with mayonnaise and put a blob in each tart. Place a piece of pastrami on top followed by the sliced pickled cucumber.

Cook's tip: Put crusts in a food processor to make breadcrumbs and store in freezer until needed.

SEARED TUNA IN A TORTILLA WRAP WITH CORN AND MANGO SALSA

8 tuna steaks – each approx 175g (6oz) in weight

2 garlic cloves – crushed

juice 1 lime

1 tbsp olive oil

salt and pepper

8 large tortillas

SALSA

1 small mango – peeled and cut into tiny cubes

1 tin (195g) sweet corn

1 red pepper – de-seeded and chopped

4 heaped tbsp mayonnaise

juice 1 lime

salt and pepper

❀ Tuna is one of my favourite fish and is best seared (browned quickly at a high temperature) as it retains it juices and stays moist. It can be cooked on a barbecue, griddle or grilled.

Mix tuna steaks with crushed garlic, lime juice, olive oil, salt and pepper and leave to marinate for at least 30 minutes.

To make salsa - mix all salsa ingredients together.

☀ May be prepared up to this stage earlier in the day.

Pre-heat a barbecue, grill or griddle to maximum. Warm the tortillas by wrapping them in foil and either put in oven: 190°C, 375°F, Gas Mark 5 for 10 minutes or place on the side of the barbecue to warm. Cook tuna for 2-3 minutes on each side, basting with the marinade.

To serve – wrap tuna in tortillas and serve with salsa.

Cook's tip: It is important that the tuna isn't over cooked. The cooking times given will leave the tuna rare in the middle. If you like it slightly less rare, then cook it for a further couple of minutes on each side.

CAESAR SALAD WITH ANCHOVIES AND PARMESAN SHAVINGS

Every time I eat a Caesar salad I'm amazed at how good it tastes. It's a real classic which is always popular. Read on and you'll find my less classic but speedy way of making it.

Wash and dry the lettuce. Put the leaves in a large salad bowl (tear the larger ones in half). Make the Parmesan shavings with a potato peeler and add to lettuce with anchovies (cut in half), and croutons. Pour over dressing then toss well.

Cook's tip: You will find Caesar salad dressing available from most large supermarkets.

2 cos lettuces or other crisp lettuce

100g (3½oz) piece of Parmesan

1 tin anchovies – drained

1 packet (100g) garlic croutons ("Philleas Fogg – Mignons Morceaux" recommended)

8 tbsp Caesar Salad dressing

SWEET POTATO SALAD WITH A PARSLEY DRESSING

Sweet potatoes are very popular in the States and they make a pleasant change to the usual potato salad. This salad can be eaten hot, warm or at room temperature.

Peel potatoes, cut into cubes, about 2.5cm (1") and plunge into cold water until ready to cook. Drain and plunge potatoes into boiling water for 10 minutes or until just tender but still firm. Drain well and toss in oil and balsamic vinegar. If serving hot, toss in chopped parsley and serve. If serving cold, add the chopped parsley just before serving.

☀ May be made earlier in the day if serving cold.

Cook's tip: Be careful not to over cook the potatoes as they will go "mushy" and make sure you drain them well.

1.5kg (3lbs 5oz) sweet potatoes

8 tbsp olive oil

2 tbsp balsamic vinegar

2 handfuls fresh parsley – chopped

salt and pepper

PEANUT BUTTER AND CHOCOLATE CHEESECAKE

If you've ever tried "Reeses" (Canadian chocolates filled with peanut butter) and liked them, then you'll love this cheesecake. It's lighter than an average cheesecake but still quite rich and totally scrumptious.

You will need a spring-form cake tin, 24cm (9½") in diameter. Roughly crush biscuits and melt butter. Mix together and push into the base of the tin. Put in fridge while preparing filling. Beat cream cheese, peanut butter and icing sugar together. Break chocolate into squares and melt either in a bowl over a pan of simmering water or microwave on medium for 2½ - 3 minutes or until melted. Stir into cream cheese mixture. Whisk cream until thick and fold into mixture. Put into biscuit lined cake tin and put in fridge to chill for at least 1 hour.

200g (7oz) chocolate chip biscuits

50g (2oz) butter

200g (7oz) cream cheese ("light" cream cheese may be used)

4 heaped tbsp crunchy peanut butter

4 tbsp icing sugar

100g (3 ½oz) dark chocolate

300ml (½pt) double or whipping cream

100g (3½oz) chocolate coated raisins

◑ May be made the day before.

✳ May be frozen.

To serve – slide a flat knife around the edge of the tin and remove the sides. Sprinkle chocolate coated raisins on top. May be served with vanilla ice cream.

ORDER OF PREPARATION IF MAKING IN ADVANCE:

The day before:
1. Make mini tarts up to ◑
2. Make cheesecake.

Earlier on the day:
3. Marinate tuna and make salsa.
4. Make potato salad.

In the evening:
5. Prepare Caesar salad and toss in dressing just before serving.
6. Fill mini tarts.
7. Cook tuna.

ORDER OF PREPARATION IN UNDER 90 MINUTES:

1. Make cheesecake.
2. Marinate tuna and make salsa.
3. Make mini tarts and fill before serving.
4. Make potato salad.
5. Make Caesar salad.

MARRAKECH EXPRESS – BARBECUE

*T*his menu is ideal for easy entertaining such as barbecues as virtually all of it can be prepared in advance. It can also be cooked in the oven if you prefer and is suitable to serve at any time of the year.

SPINACH AND CHICK PEA PÂTÉ WITH EASTERN FLAT BREAD

500g (1lb 2oz) frozen spinach – de-frosted and drained

2 tins (400g each) chick peas – drained

200g (7oz) cream cheese

2 large handfuls raisins

4 level tsp cumin seeds

3 - 4 level tsp harissa paste – optional

salt and pepper

4 large or 8 small naan (or 8 small pitta bread)

olive oil

This pâté, made out of all the traditional ingredients found in Morocco, can be made hot and spicy by the addition of harissa. Harissa is a fiery North African paste made out of chillies, garlic and spices pounded together. Add as much or as little as you like.

Put all ingredients, except the naan, in a food processor and pulse the mixture a few times so that it is mixed together to a coarse consistency. Either put into a large serving bowl or into 8 individual ramekin dishes.

❋ May be made the day before or may be frozen.

Lightly brush both sides of the naan or pitta bread with olive oil and put on the barbecue to warm. Alternatively you can wrap the naan or pitta in silver foil and put in oven: 190°C, 375°F, Gas Mark 5 for 10 minutes.

Serve the warm naan with the pâté.

Cook's tip: The pâté will have quite a soft consistency so it can also be served as a dip.

MOROCCAN SPICED LAMB

1 whole leg lamb – butterflied, i.e. take out the bone, leaving two flaps – cut off excess fat

4 red onions – peeled and cut into quarters

8 courgettes – cut in half

2 lemons – cut in quarters

MARINADE

2 level tsp each of paprika, turmeric, ground ginger, ground coriander, cumin (seeds or powder)

4 garlic cloves – chopped or crushed

4 tbsp olive oil

juice 1 lemon

salt and pepper

Oven: 200°C, 400°F, Gas Mark 6

Butterflied lamb is delicious cooked on the barbecue. I prefer to start it off in the oven and then transfer it to the barbecue. This method ensures that it is cooked through but it can also be cooked entirely on the barbecue, or entirely in the oven, if you prefer. In every case the cooking time is 50-60 minutes.

Mix all marinade ingredients together. Put the lamb in a non-metallic bowl or dish with half the marinade and add the other half of the marinade to the onions, courgettes and lemons in another dish. Leave to marinate for at least 1 hour or overnight.

◗ May be prepared up to this stage the day before.

Light the barbecue. Cook lamb in oven for 25 - 30 minutes and then transfer to the barbecue for 25 - 30 minutes, basting regularly with the marinade and turning every now and then. Cook vegetables and lemon on the barbecue for 20 minutes, basting with the marinade or cook in the oven with marinade for 40 minutes. Slice the lamb thickly and serve with vegetables, lemons and any remaining marinade.

Cooks tip: The cooking time of the lamb will depend on whether you like it well done or pink in the middle.

COUSCOUS WITH PISTACHIO NUTS AND CORIANDER

The type of couscous now available in the shops has been partially cooked, making couscous an almost instant dish, to which you can add nuts, herbs, vegetables and a whole variety of different ingredients.

400g (14oz) couscous

850ml (1½pts) lamb, chicken or vegetable stock – made with one stock cube and boiling water

100g (3½oz) shelled pistachio nuts

2 handfuls chopped coriander

salt and pepper

Pour hot stock onto couscous. Leave to soak for 10 minutes. Fork the couscous to break up any lumps and add pistachio nuts, salt and pepper. Either serve immediately with chopped coriander stirred in or leave to cool and re-heat.

◑ May be prepared the day before.

To re-heat – put in microwave on high for 5 minutes until hot through and stir in chopped coriander.

Cooks tip: To save washing up, prepare this in its serving dish.

BRANDY MACERATED FIGS AND DATES WITH HONEYED YOGHURT

Moroccans tend to eat fruit and nuts at the end of a meal rather than desserts. They do love sweet things and often eat them during the day with mint tea. Figs and dates are favourites in Morocco so I have used them to make this delicious brandy drenched dessert.

500g (1lb 2oz) dried figs

250g (9oz) dried, stoned dates

2 tsp cinnamon

8 tbsp brandy

8 tbsp orange juice

500g (1lb 2oz) Greek yoghurt

3 tbsp runny honey

Mix together figs, dates, cinnamon, brandy and orange juice. Leave to marinate for as long as possible – in fact they can be kept in the fridge for up to one week.

Mix Greek yoghurt with honey and refrigerate until needed.

◑ May be prepared the day before or even the week before.

Serve figs and dates with yoghurt.

ORDER OF PREPARATION IF MAKING IN ADVANCE:

1. Make pâté.
2. Marinate lamb and vegetables.
3. Make couscous.
4. Make pudding.

   In the evening:
5. Cook lamb and vegetables as necessary.
6. Warm naan or pitta.
7. Re-heat couscous.

ORDER OF PREPARATION IN UNDER 90 MINUTES:

1. Marinate lamb and vegetables for as long as possible and cook as needed.
2. Make pâté and warm naan or pitta as needed.
3. Make pudding.
4. Make couscous.

A MOVEABLE FEAST

Wonderfully elegant picnics that you might take to Ascot or Glyndebourne are great fun but there are also times when you just want to pack the minimum and leave the candelabra at home together with the kitchen sink. This picnic is a real feast, can be transported in foil and cling-film, be eaten in fingers and best of all, no washing up afterwards. In fact all you need to take with you is a pen knife with a good cork screw to open the wine. It's ideal for eating on a beach, in a boat, on a fishing trip, or even in the back garden.

ASPARAGUS IN PROSCIUTTO WRAPS

Perfect to eat in your fingers. The prosciutto and cream cheese are wrapped around the middle of the asparagus leaving the tips and ends "unwrapped".

32 asparagus pieces – approx 700g (1½ lbs)
100g (3½ oz) cream cheese
160g (6oz) prosciutto or 11 slices

Cut the woody ends off the asparagus and plunge into boiling water for 4-6 minutes until tender. Drain and rinse in cold water to cool. Spread cream cheese over the prosciutto slices and cut each slice into three. Lay a piece of asparagus on top and roll up, repeating until you have used up all the asparagus. Wrap in cling-film.

◑ May be prepared the day before.

TUNA AND SUN-DRIED TOMATO FISH CAKES

These fish cakes are delicious eaten on their own or dipped into the wild herb aioli.

2 tins (400g each) tuna – drained
½ jar ((90g) sun-dried tomato paste
1 tub (200ml) crème fraîche – the half fat type may be used
1 bunch spring onions – thinly sliced
5 heaped tbsp breadcrumbs (taken from inside of bread bowl)
4 eggs – beaten
salt and pepper
Oven: 220°C, 425°F, Gas Mark 7

Grease two baking trays. Mix all ingredients together. Allowing a heaped tablespoon per fish cake, put 24 "blobs" on the baking trays. Cook for 6 minutes on each side – they will still look gungy when you turn them over but don't worry. May be eaten immediately or left to cool and eaten cold.

◑ May be made the day before. Wrap in cling-film or foil.

Cook's tip: This mixture will be quite sloppy but will go more solid when it is cooked.

WILD HERB AND AIOLI DIP IN A BREAD BOWL

1 round Pain de Campagne

2 handfuls parsley

2 handfuls basil

4 handfuls rocket

3 garlic cloves

juice of 1 lemon

400ml (¾pt) mayonnaise

salt and pepper

The amount of herbs and garlic in this dip make it really wild. It's handy serving it in an edible bowl which can be frozen and will also act as an ice pack to keep everything cool.

Cut a lid from the loaf and hollow out the base. Put the scooped out bread into a food processor to make breadcrumbs for fish cakes. The hollowed loaf and lid can be kept in the freezer until needed.

To make dip put herbs, garlic and lemon juice in a food processor to blend. Put into a bowl, add mayonnaise and season.

◗ May be prepared a day or two before.

Take bread bowl out of freezer and fill with dip. Wrap tightly in foil or cling-film. The frozen bread bowl will help to keep the dip and surrounding food cold. The bowl can be eaten later.

Cook's tip: Make breadcrumbs before making dip then you won't need to wash the food processor up in between.

GREEN CRUDITÉS AND NEW POTATOES

1kg (2lbs 4oz) new potatoes

250g (9oz) sugar snap peas

2 green peppers

2 gem lettuce

3 heads chicory

This looks really effective just using vegetables which are the same colour. I would suggest using a contrasting brightly coloured tea towel to serve them on to show up the green of the crudités.

Cook new potatoes in boiling water for about 15 minutes or until tender. Drain, rinse in cold water and leave to cool. Top and tail sugar snap peas, de-seed peppers and cut into strips. Store green vegetables in polythene bags in the fridge.

◗ May be prepared up to this stage the day before.

To serve – separate the leaves of gem lettuce and chicory. Arrange all vegetables, including new potatoes, on a clean colourful tea towel and serve with bread bowl and dip.

CITRUS AND ALMOND "GUNGE" CAKE
WITH FRESH STRAWBERRIES

1 large orange - cut into 4
zest and juice of 1 lemon
zest and juice of 1 lime
100g (3½oz) butter
100g (3½oz) caster sugar
200g (7oz) ground almonds
2 tsp baking powder
500g (1lb 2oz) strawberries
Oven: 190°C, 375°F, Gas Mark 5

This is an ideal cake to take on a picnic as it feels firm but tastes wonderfully moist and light. It doesn't have any flour in it so is ideal for Coeliacs and people on a wheat-free diet.

Grease a spring-form or loose bottomed cake tin, 24cm (9½") in diameter. Cut out a circle of baking parchment to line the base of the tin. Put all ingredients including skin and pith of orange but excluding strawberries in a food processor until smooth. Tip into cake tin and put in oven for 30 minutes. Leave to stand in cake tin for 10 minutes, then turn out onto a wire rack to cool.

Slide a flat knife around the edge of the tin and remove sides and base. Cut into squares.

◐ May be made the day before.

✳ May be frozen.

Serve with strawberries.

Cook's tip: This cake is also delicious eaten warm (but not on a picnic). To re-heat – leave cake whole and put back in oven: 190°C, 375°F, Gas Mark 5 for 15 minutes. Dust with icing sugar and serve with fromage frais or Greek yoghurt.

ORDER OF PREPARATION IF MAKING IN ADVANCE:

The day before:
1. Make citrus cake.
2. Make bread bowl and dip
3. Make tuna fish cakes.
4. Make asparagus in wraps.
5. Prepare vegetables for crudités.

On the day.
6. Fill bread bowl with dip.

ORDER OF PREPARATION IN UNDER 90 MINUTES:
Same as above.

MYSTERY MUSTIQUE

♀ *An aromatic, spicy white.*
Recommendation – Cono Sur
Gewürztraminer from Chile

*T*his menu is really a mixture of Caribbean and Cajun cooking. Cajun cuisine, coming from the American deep south, is very similar to that of the Caribbean Islands with an abundance of fish and tangy spices. It all seems very mysterious and you'll be amazed how you can create such an exotic dinner party in cloudy old England.

CHILLED SPICY TOMATO, CLAM AND CELERY SOUP WITH WARM CORN CHIPS

This lovely chilled, spicy soup is ideal for a warm summer evening but can also be served hot for those colder days.

1 litre (1¾ pts) tomato juice
2 tins (400g each) chopped tomatoes
2 tins (290g each) clams – drained
5 sticks celery – thinly sliced – reserve leaves to chop for decoration
4 spring onions – chopped
juice of ½ a lemon
2 tbsp Worcester sauce
1 tsp celery salt
Tabasco or chilli sauce to taste
1 large bag corn or tortilla chips

Mix all ingredients, except corn/tortilla chips, together and chill.

◗ May be made the day before.

To warm corn/tortilla chips - put on a baking tray and put in oven: 180°C, 350°F, Gas Mark 4 for 10 minutes.

To serve – put soup into bowls and sprinkle chopped celery leaves on top.

Cook's tips: The corn/tortilla chips may also be served cold straight from the packet. To chill the soup quickly, add a few ice cubes.

SWORDFISH WITH CAJUN SPICES AND A KIWI AND CUCUMBER SALSA

This is also known as "blackened fish" as it is usually briefly charred over an extremely hot griddle and gives a blackened effect. I find it easier when entertaining to cook the fish in the oven and be able to forget about it for 20 minutes. This recipe also works well on a barbecue.

8 swordfish steaks (approx 175g/6oz each)
6 tsp Cajun seasoning
2 limes – cut into wedges
SALSA
4 kiwi fruit – peeled and chopped
½ cucumber – chopped but not peeled
4 spring onions – thinly sliced
1 green chilli – de-seeded and chopped
juice of ½ a lime
Oven: 220°C, 425°F, Gas Mark 7

Coat swordfish in the Cajun seasoning. Mix all salsa ingredients together.

☼ May be prepared up to this point earlier in the day.

Grease an oven tray and put fish on top. Cook in oven for 20 minutes and serve with salsa and lime wedges.

Cook's tip: Cajun seasoning is now widely available in most large supermarkets. If you are unable to find it, make it up yourself by mixing together: 1 tsp chilli powder, 1 tsp ground ginger, 1 tsp allspice and 1 tsp ground coriander.

GREEN BEAN, BANANA, CASHEW AND COCONUT SALAD

600g (1lb 5oz) French beans

8 tbsp ready-made French dressing

1 cos lettuce – shredded

100g (3½oz) unsalted cashew nuts

3 bananas – peeled and sliced

4 tbsp desiccated coconut

salt and pepper

This sounds unusual but you will find the banana and desiccated coconut give this salad a really tropical taste.

Top and tail French beans and cook in boiling water for around 7 minutes or until tender. Drain and toss in dressing while still hot. Leave to cool.

✵ May be prepared up to this point earlier in the day.

Toss all ingredients in a large salad bowl.

Cook's tip: Slice and add the bananas just before serving to stop them going brown.

STUFFED BAKED SWEET POTATOES

4 sweet potatoes – weighing 350g-400g (12oz-14oz) each

zest and juice of 1 orange

2 handfuls fresh chopped coriander

Oven: 220°C, 425°F, Gas Mark 7

Sweet potatoes are part of the staple diet in the Caribbean. They go deliciously buttery and nutty when baked and, unlike ordinary potatoes, don't need the addition of extra butter or margarine.

Scrub the potatoes well and cook in oven for 45 minutes – 1 hour or until tender. Cut in half and slightly mash with a fork but keep halves intact. Mix in orange zest, juice and half the coriander. Put back in oven for 10 minutes and scatter remaining coriander on top. Allow half a sweet potato per person.

✵ May be prepared earlier in the day but, once stuffed, do not put back in the oven until 15 minutes before you need them. This will heat them up from cold.

SWEET TORTILLA SHELLS WITH PINEAPPLE AND MALIBU ICE CREAM

8 small wheat tortillas

4 tbsp icing sugar

1 medium sized pineapple

1 tub (500g) Malibu Ice Cream – (see Cook's tip)

large slug rum (approx 4 tbsp)

Oven: 180°C, 350°F, Gas Mark 4

Why are tortillas always served as a savoury? Well, I couldn't think of any reason why so have come up with this sweet version. They are simply baked, using a bowl to mould them in, and filled with wonderful tropical goodies.

You will need to use oven-proof bowls, anything from 12cm-14cm (4½ - 5½") in diameter, as moulds for the tortilla shells. Put the tortillas into the bowls, sprinkle with half the icing sugar and put in oven for 15 minutes. You may have to do this in batches if you don't have 8 bowls. Allow to cool. Peel the pineapple, cut into 8 slices and cut the slices in quarters. Put in a bowl with the rum.

◗ May be made up to this point the day before and the tortilla shells may be kept in an air-tight container for up to 2 days.

To serve – fill each tortilla shell with a scoop of ice cream, 4 pieces of pineapple, rum and juices from the pineapple and sprinkle with remaining icing sugar.

Cook's tip: "Haagan Dazs" make scrummy Malibu ice cream but you can also use rum and raisin or coconut if you prefer.

ORDER OF PREPARATION IF MAKING
IN ADVANCE:

The day before:
1. Make the soup.
2. Make tortilla shell recipe up to ◖

Earlier on the day:
3. Season the swordfish and make salsa.
4. Make bean salad up to ☼
5. Bake sweet potatoes.

In the evening:
6. Cook swordfish.
7. Warm corn chips.
8. Put sweet potatoes back in oven to heat.
9. Finish off bean salad.

ORDER OF PREPARATION IN UNDER
90 MINUTES:

1. Make soup and chill. Warm corn chips before serving.
2. Cook sweet potatoes.
3. Prepare sword fish and salsa and cook as needed.
4. Prepare bean salad up to ☼ and finish off just before serving.
5. Make tortilla shells and prepare pineapple – assemble before serving.

NO COOK INDIAN

♀ A soft, warm red.
Recommendation – Portada
from Portugal

What do you do if you have 8 people coming round and your oven isn't working or it's so hot you can't face cooking? Answer: Make the following.

PRAWN, AVOCADO AND MANGO WITH POPPADOMS

Avocado with prawns take on a new slant with this recipe. The addition of fresh mango and mango chutney gives an old favourite that Delhi feeling!

2 avocados
400g (14oz) cooked, shelled prawns
juice of ½ lemon
4 tbsp mango chutney
2 tbsp mayonnaise
1 mango
1 handful fresh chopped coriander
8 ready-to-eat poppadoms

Peel and roughly chop the avocado. Mix with lemon juice, prawns, mango chutney and mayonnaise. Peel and slice the mango.

☀ May be prepared earlier in the day.

Arrange the mango slices on individual serving plates. Pile the avocado and prawn mixture in the middle, and sprinkle chopped coriander on top. Serve with poppadoms.

CHICKEN TIKKA AND LIME KEBABS WITH SPINACH AND MINT RAITA

These days you can buy ready cooked chicken tikka or tandoori pieces. They look impressive threaded onto kebab sticks and are complimented by the cool, refreshing raita.

900g (2lbs) chicken tikka pieces (tandoori chicken may be used instead)
2 limes – each cut into 8 wedges
1 cucumber – cut into 16 thick slices
SPINACH AND MINT RAITA
250g (9oz) frozen chopped spinach – defrosted and drained
500g (1lb 2oz) plain yoghurt
1 red onion – finely sliced
2 tsp cumin seeds or powder
2 handfuls fresh chopped mint
salt and pepper

Mix all raita ingredients together.

◖ May be prepared the day before

For the kebabs you will need 8 long wooden or metal kebab sticks. Either leave the chicken pieces whole or cut them in half if they are large. Thread them onto the kebab sticks alternating with wedges of lime and slices of cucumber.

☀ May be prepared earlier in the day.

Serve kebabs with raita.

CURRIED LENTILS AND BULGUR WHEAT

 Bulgur wheat is ideal in this menu as it needs no cooking and has a lovely nutty, crunchy texture.

1 (400g) tin lentils – drained

225g (8oz) bulgur wheat

400ml (14fl oz) water

3 tsp curry powder

juice ½ lemon

salt and pepper

4 tbsp olive oil

Mix all ingredients together except the olive oil and leave to soak for 1 hour.

◖ May be prepared up to this stage the day before.

Mix with olive oil and serve.

CARROT, SULTANA AND CORIANDER SALAD WITH AN ORANGE AND GINGER DRESSING

 This salad is wonderfully light, fruity and healthy.

800g (1lb 12oz) carrots – grated

3 handfuls sultanas

1 bunch spring onions – sliced

2 handfuls fresh chopped coriander

juice of 1 orange

2 tsp ground ginger

salt and pepper

Mix all ingredients together.

☼ May be prepared earlier in the day.

Cook's tip: Grate the carrots in a food processor to save time.

THE AMAZING BANANA PAVLOVA

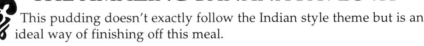 This pudding doesn't exactly follow the Indian style theme but is an ideal way of finishing off this meal.

1 packet ready-made meringues
(6-8 meringues)

2 litres good quality vanilla ice cream

4 bananas – sliced

100g (3½oz) dark chocolate – grated

butterscotch sauce (Smuckers
recommended) or maple syrup

Roughly crush the meringues but leave in quite large pieces. Spread out on a large platter. Just before serving, scoop ice cream on top, followed by sliced bananas. Scatter with chocolate and dribble with butterscotch sauce or maple syrup.

ORDER OF PREPARATION IF MAKING IN ADVANCE:

The day before:
1. Make raita.
2. Make curried lentils and bulgur wheat up to ◖

Earlier on the day:
3. Make starter up to ☼
4. Make the kebabs.
5. Make carrot salad.

In the evening:
6. Mix the olive oil into the lentils and bulgur wheat.
7. Assemble the Pavlova just before serving.

And nothing else apart from putting things on plates!

ORDER OF PREPARATION IN UNDER 90 MINUTES:

1. Make lentils and bulgur wheat up to ◖ and add olive oil before serving.
2. Make raita and prepare kebabs.
3. Make carrot salad.
4. Make starter.
5. Assemble pudding just before serving.

A PENNE FOR YOUR THOUGHTS
(Vegetarian)

♉ New World Sauvignon Blanc.
Recommendation – Montana
Sauvignon Blanc from New Zealand

Penne (pronounced peni) is short wide tubular pasta. A penny for your thoughts – a request from a thoughtful person to confide in the speaker – but you won't have to give this menu much thought. It's so easy to provide a meatless meal without anyone feeling deprived – thanks to pasta.

1.3kg (3lbs) thick asparagus

8 tsp black olive tapenade
(see Cook's tips)

10 tbsp olive oil

200g bag mixed salad leaves

GARLIC BREAD STICKS

½ large white sandwich tin loaf

50g (2oz) butter

2 garlic cloves – crushed

salt and pepper

Oven: 200°C, 400°F, Gas Mark 6

ASPARAGUS WITH BLACK OLIVE TAPENADE AND GARLIC BREAD STICKS

❦ We now seem to be able to buy imported asparagus all year round but I still think that our British asparagus is the best and is usually available between May and August. It comes in many different sizes and, for this recipe, I like to use the thicker ones and allow about 6-8 pieces per person. Rather than boiling or steaming the asparagus, I grill or griddle them so that they retain their crunch, flavour and shape.

Either heat a grill or griddle pan. Trim off the rough ends of the asparagus and brush with 2 tbsp olive oil. Grill or griddle for approximately 6 minutes, turning the asparagus half way through, or until tender but still crunchy. Mix black olive tapenade with remaining 8 tbsp olive oil and pour over asparagus while still hot. Either serve immediately or leave to marinate and serve at room temperature.

◗ May be made up to this point the day before.

To make the garlic bread sticks – cut the crusts from the bread so that you are left with a large cube. Cut into 4 thick slices (approx 2.5cm/1" thick) and cut each slice into 4 sticks. Put on a baking tray in one layer. Melt butter, mix with garlic, season and pour over the bread sticks. Put in oven for 15 minutes, turning half way through, until golden. They should resemble fish fingers when cooked!

To serve – arrange leaves on each plate and put asparagus with tapenade on top. Serve with garlic bread sticks.

Cook's tips: Black olive tapenade or paste is available from major supermarkets and delis. It can be substituted by sun-dried tomato paste if preferred. The cooking time of the asparagus will vary depending on the thickness so you will have to test it by sticking the point of a knife in or, better still, eating a piece yourself.

PENNE PASTA WITH ROAST VEGETABLES, PINE NUTS AND CHÈVRE

This is one of my favourite recipes in the book. It contains all my favourite ingredients – pasta, roast vegetables, pine nuts and chèvre – heaven. I have used penne (tubular shapes, quills) but other types may be used – see Cook's tip below.

Put all ingredients up to the tinned tomatoes into a large roasting dish (you may need 2) and roast in oven for 50 minutes, tossing half way through. Add tinned tomatoes, sugar, chèvre, black olives, salt and pepper, toss and put back in oven for a further 10 minutes. Cook the penne as instructions on the packet and toss together with the vegetables. Either put into a huge serving bowl and decorate with remaining basil leaves or serve on individual plates.

Cook's tip: Other types of pasta may be used e.g. tagliatelle, fusilli (spirals), farfalle (bows).

1 large aubergine – cut into chunks

6 courgettes – sliced

6 tomatoes – cut in quarters

2 red onions – peeled and cut in eighths

2 red and 2 yellow peppers – de-seeded and cut into large slices

4 garlic cloves – sliced

3 handfuls basil – shred 2 handfuls and reserve the rest for decoration

100g (3½oz) pine nuts

4 tbsp olive oil

2 tins (400g each) chopped tomatoes in onion and olive oil or plain tomatoes

2 tsp sugar

4 rounds chèvre (approx 400g (14oz) in total) – cut into quarters

1 jar black olives (optional)

1kg (2lbs 4oz) penne – fresh or dried

salt and pepper

Oven: 220°C, 425°F, Gas Mark 7

ARTICHOKE AND BORLOTTI BEAN SALAD

These oval pinky-brown beans are from Italy and give a lovely bitter-sweet flavour.

In a large salad bowl mix borlotti beans, artichokes including the oil, balsamic vinegar and season together.

☼ May be prepared earlier in the day.

Add lamb's lettuce just before serving and toss.

1 tin (400g) borlotti beans - drained

1 jar (280g) artichoke hearts in oil – each cut in ½

3 tbsp balsamic vinegar

300g (10oz) lamb's lettuce or other salad leaves

salt and pepper

ICED LEMON MERINGUE AND VODKA MOUSSE

100g (3½oz) ginger nut biscuits

4 heaped tbsp lemon curd

500g (1lb 2oz) Greek yoghurt

a very large slug vodka – at least 4 tbsp or more to taste

1 packet meringue nests (containing 6-8 meringues)

 This is a lovely refreshing dessert to finish off the meal. The amount of vodka you put in is discretionary but I would suggest a lot!

Roughly crush the ginger nut biscuits by putting them in a polythene bag, sealing the end, and bashing them with a rolling pin. Divide between 8 glasses or ramekin dishes. Mix lemon curd, Greek yoghurt and vodka together. Roughly crush the meringues – leave in packet and bash with your fist. Fold into yoghurt mixture and put on top of ginger nut biscuits. Put in freezer for at least 1 hour.

❄ May be kept in freezer for up to 2 months.

Cook's tip: This can be served directly from the freezer as the vodka will stop the mousse becoming too solid.

ORDER OF PREPARATION IF MAKING IN ADVANCE:

The day before:
1. Prepare asparagus up to ◑
2. Make lemon mousse.

Earlier in the day:
3. Prepare salad up to ❄

In the evening:
4. Prepare everything for pasta recipe and cook as needed.
5. Prepare garlic bread sticks, put in oven as needed and arrange asparagus on plates.
6. Toss salad ingredients together just before serving.

ORDER OF PREPARATION IN UNDER 90 MINUTES:

1. Make lemon mousse.
2. Prepare pasta recipe and cook as needed.
3. Prepare salad and add lamb's lettuce just before serving.
4. Prepare and cook garlic bread sticks and asparagus.

A SMART SUPPER IN ADVANCE

♀ *An oaky, Australian white.*
Recommendation – W.W. Chardonnay
from Australia

*D*o you ever find that you've been busy all day, arranged an early evening game of tennis, golf, theatre, school play, etc. with friends and have also invited them back for dinner afterwards? Do you then worry how you're ever going to manage to produce a wonderful meal in no time at all? Well, don't panic – this is the ideal menu which you can prepare in advance, and freeze if you wish, so that you have a virtually instant gourmet meal waiting for you when you get home.

WARM COURGETTE TIMBALES WITH RED PEPPER MARMALADE

oil for greasing

650g (1lb 7oz) courgettes –
or approx. 4 large ones

200g (7oz) cream cheese

2 eggs

salt and pepper

RED PEPPER MARMALADE

2 tbsp olive oil

2 red peppers – de-seeded and
thinly sliced

1 red onion – sliced

2 heaped tbsp thick cut marmalade

Oven: 200°C, 400°F, Gas Mark 6

This is a real wow to impress your friends – they'll find it difficult to believe that you can produce this in a matter of minutes.

Brush 8 ramekin dishes with oil. Cut the courgettes into thick chunks and put in a food processor with cream cheese, eggs, salt and pepper to blend. Put into ramekins and put in oven for 20 minutes.

Meanwhile, make red pepper marmalade. Heat the olive oil in a saucepan, add peppers and onion and cook gently over a low heat with the lid on for 10 minutes. Add marmalade and continue to cook for a further 5 minutes, stirring occasionally. If serving immediately, slide a flat knife round the sides of each ramekin, turn out on to individual plates and serve with red pepper marmalade. If making in advance, leave to cool in ramekins.

◐ May be prepared the day before.

✳ The courgette timbales may be frozen.

To re-heat – turn out of ramekins and put on an oiled baking tray in oven for 10 minutes. For the red pepper marmalade either re-heat in saucepan or put in microwave on high for 3 minutes.

Cook's tip: If you are going to freeze the timbales, I would suggest turning them out of the ramekins first so that you can use the ramekins for other things in the meantime.

THREE SALMON KEDGEREE WITH WILD RICE AND QUAILS' EGGS

This is a lovely unusual kedgeree which is very versatile as it can be served for a smart supper, brunch, lunch or any time of the day. I have used quails' eggs for a change, but don't worry about peeling them – it's much too time consuming – let your guests do it themselves.

3tbsp olive oil
1 large onion – chopped
400g (14oz) basmati and wild rice – "Tilda" recommended
1.2lt (2pts) fish stock – use 2 fish stock cubes and boiling water
600g (1lb 5oz) fresh salmon fillets – skinnned – cut into chunks
16 quails' eggs – hard boiled
100g (3½oz) gravalax – cut into strips
100g (3½oz) smoked salmon – cut into strips
2½ lemons
3 handfuls fresh dill – chop 2 handfuls and reserve 1 for decoration
salt and pepper

Heat the olive oil in a very large saucepan, add the chopped onion and fry gently for 5 minutes to soften. Add rice, stir to coat in oil, and add hot stock, bring up to the boil and simmer for 10 minutes. Add fresh salmon and leave to simmer for a further 10 minutes until rice is tender and liquid is absorbed. If making in advance add other ingredients when re-heating – see instructions below. Add gravalax, smoked salmon, juice of ½ lemon, 2 handfuls chopped dill and season. Leave to heat through for a few minutes. See serving instructions below.

◑ May be prepared the day before.

✳ May be frozen.

To re-heat – de-frost if necessary, put in an oven-proof serving dish and mix in the gravalax, smoked salmon, juice of ½ lemon , 2 handfuls chopped dill and season. Cover and put in oven: 190°C, 375°F, Gas Mark 5 for 35 minutes or microwave on high for 12 minutes, stirring half way through.

To serve – cut remaining lemons into wedges. Put kedgeree onto a serving dish and put the lemon wedges round the edge of the dish together with the quails' eggs (unpeeled) and remaining dill.

Cook's tip: It is important that the kedgeree should be nice and moist. If you are making the kedgeree in advance and you think it is becoming dry, add some more fish stock.

CHERRY TOMATO AND WATERCRESS SALAD WITH AN ELDERFLOWER DRESSING

This salad is easier to make than it sounds. Now that you can buy elderflower cordial, there's no need to pick the elderflowers yourself and squeeze the juice out of them. They bring a lovely sweet fragrance to this salad.

500g (1lb 2oz) cherry tomatoes – cut in half
2 bunches watercress or 2 (75g) bags
DRESSING:
5 tbsp olive oil
3 tbsp elderflower cordial
salt and pepper

Mix dressing ingredients together.

◑ May be made in advance and kept in the fridge for a few days.

Put tomatoes and watercress into a salad bowl and toss with dressing.

DOUBLE BOURBON ICED TERRINE WITH RASPBERRIES AND A MAPLE PECAN SAUCE

1 litre good quality ice cream

1 packet (200g) bourbon biscuits

large slug bourbon or whisky
(approx 4 tbsp)

150ml (¼pt) maple syrup

100g (3½oz) pecans

400g (14oz) raspberries

This is a wonderful pudding for all age groups. I have tested this recipe out on various friends and family, ranging in age from a 91 year old aunt to my 8 year old twins. It has proved to be a real success with both plus anyone aged in-between.

Line a 1 litre terrine dish with cling-film. Allow ice cream to slightly soften. Roughly crush biscuits by leaving them in the packet and bashing them with rolling pin. Mix with ice cream and whisky. Put into terrine tin and put in freezer.

Cook's tip: As an alternative idea, this could also be served with a chocolate sauce and raspberries.

ORDER OF PREPARATION IF MAKING IN ADVANCE:

The day before:
1. Make starter.
2. Prepare kedgeree up to ◗
3. Make dressing for salad.
4. Make bourbon terrine.

In the evening:
1. Re-heat starter and kedgeree.
2. Make salad.

ORDER OF PREPARATION IN UNDER 90 MINUTES:

1. Make bourbon terrine.
2. Prepare starter and re-heat if necessary.
3. Make kedgeree.
4. Make salad.

TRULY TROPICAL

♀ *A ripe New World white. Recommendation - Vina Porta Chardonnay from Chile*

*T*his menu is full of tropical flavours and spices to conjure up images of sun-drenched beaches, blue seas, palm trees and relaxing with a Pina Colada or a glass of Chilean Chardonnay.

AVOCADO AND RED KIDNEY BEAN DIP WITH TORTILLA CHIPS

1 large packet tortilla chips

1 large packet "Blue Corn" tortilla chips

DIP

1 green chilli – de-seeded

½ a red onion

1 tin (400g) red kidney beans – drained

1 avocado

2 tbsp mayonnaise

juice of 1 lemon plus 1 lemon for decoration cut into wedges

salt and pepper

I have suggested using a mixture of the usual gold coloured tortilla chips and black chips (called "blue corn"). The blue corn chips are available from most large supermarkets and delis but if you cannot find them, use just gold ones or see other suggestions in Cook's tip below.

Put chilli into a food processor and chop finely. Add all remaining dip ingredients and pulse until mixed together but not too smooth.

◑ May be prepared the day before.

Serve dip in a bowl, decorated with lemon wedges. Put on a large platter and arrange tortilla chips around the bowl.

Cook's tip: The dip may also be served with various raw vegetables, for example, carrot sticks, celery, chicory, green pepper.

TROPICAL FISH STEW WITH COCONUT MILK IN MELON BOWLS

2 small red chillies

2 garlic cloves – chopped

3 handfuls fresh coriander – chop 2 and reserve 1 for decoration

1.25kg (2lbs 12oz) firm fish steaks, e.g. tuna and swordfish – skin removed and cut into chunks – approx 2.5cm (1")

16 raw tiger prawn tails

1 tin (400ml) coconut milk

1 red pepper – de-seeded and sliced

3 tsp allspice or "Jerk" seasoning – (see Cook's tip)

1 small pineapple – peeled, sliced and cut in quarters

8 melon bowls – (see page 80)

Oven: 190°C., 375°F, Gas Mark 5

You need to use firm, dense fish for this recipe, so I have used a mixture of tuna, swordfish and tiger prawn tails. The red chillies add quite a bit of spiciness and if you prefer a milder flavour then I would recommend using only one chilli. It looks impressively tropical served in the melon bowls.

Put red chillies (de-seeded and chopped), garlic and 2 handfuls of coriander in a food processor or chop by hand. Mix together with all other ingredients, except coriander for decoration, and put into a large bowl or casserole dish.

◑ May be prepared the day before.

Cover and put in oven for 45 minutes – 1 hour until cooked through.
To serve – put fish stew into melon bowls and decorate with remaining coriander.

Cook's tip: Jerk seasoning is a mixture of Jamaican spices and herbs and contains chilli, cinnamon, nutmeg, marjoram and garlic. Allspice is also a mixture of Jamaican spices and works well with this recipe or you can mix the spices up yourself.

MELON AND CUCUMBER SALAD WITH A LIME AND CHIVE DRESSING

2 Galia melons

2 Charentais melons

1 cucumber

DRESSING

zest and juice of 2 limes

bunch of chives – chopped

4 tbsp ground nut oil
(or other tasteless oil)

2 tsp sugar

salt and pepper

This is a lovely refreshing salad to complement the fish stew. I have used a mixture of Galia and Charentais melons to give a contrast of colours. Try to buy melons that are similar in size as they are going to be used as bowls for the fish stew.

Mix all dressing ingredients together.

◐ May be prepared the day before.

Cut the melons in half, through the equator. Discard the seeds and, using a melon baller or teaspoon, scoop the flesh into balls and put in a salad bowl. Reserve the melon skins to use as bowls for the fish stew. Cut the cucumber into cubes, about 1cm (½"), mix with the melon and toss together with the dressing.

BROWN RICE AND BLACKEYE BEANS

1.5 litres (2¾pts) boiling water

400g (14oz) long-grain brown rice

1 fish stock cube

1 tin (400g) blackeye beans – drained

Rice with beans is very popular in the Caribbean and West Indies but is usually called "rice with peas".

Bring water up to the boil in a saucepan, add rice and stock cube and simmer for 30 minutes. Add blackeye beans and continue to simmer for a further 10 minutes or until water is absorbed and rice is tender.

Cook's tip: If you can't find tinned blackeye beans, then use cannellini beans instead.

BAKED BANANAS WITH RUM AND CINNAMON ICE CREAM

1 litre good quality vanilla ice cream

2 tsp cinnamon

8 tbsp dark rum

8 bananas

250ml (9fl oz) orange juice

3 tbsp dark muscovado sugar

Oven: 190°C, 375°F, Gas Mark 5

The pace of life is so slow and laid back in the tropics and it's probably large quantities of rum that help create this. I'm sure this pudding will help you relax!

Allow ice cream to soften slightly and mix together with cinnamon and 4 tbsp of the rum. Put into a freezer-proof serving bowl and freeze.

❋ May be kept in the freezer for up to 2 months.

Peel bananas, leave whole and put into an oven-proof serving dish in one layer. Add orange juice, sugar and remaining rum. Put in oven for 20 minutes and serve with cinnamon ice cream.

Cook's tip: The bananas can be prepared an hour or two before you are going to cook them as the orange juice will prevent them going brown. There is no need to take the ice cream out of the freezer until you are ready to serve it. As alcohol doesn't freeze, the rum will ensure that it doesn't get too solid.

Opposite: A Penne For Your Thoughts (page 73)

ORDER OF PREPARATION IF MAKING
IN ADVANCE:

The day before:
1. Prepare fish stew using food processor
   to chop chilli, garlic and coriander
   before making the dip. There's no
   need to wash it in between.
2. Make dip.
3. Make lime and chive dressing.
4. Make ice cream.

In the evening:
5. Make melon salad.
6. Cook rice.
7. Cook fish.
8 Cook bananas.

ORDER OF PREPARATION IN
UNDER 90 MINUTES:

1. Make ice cream.
2. Prepare fish stew – don't wash
   food processor.
3. Make dip.
4. Cook rice as necessary.
5. Make melon salad.
6. Cook bananas as needed.

*Opposite: Good Cod – A Wheat
and Gluten-free Feast (page 88)*

VEGETARIAN BARBECUE

♀ *A soft red to be served*
slightly chilled.
Recommendation – Normans Jesse's
Blend from Australia

Most people assume that you can only cook meat on a barbecue and often these events become a complete nightmare for vegetarians. In fact there are plenty of exciting non-meat things that taste delicious barbecued. For example, fish works well and in this menu I have used marinated halloumi – it's good enough to turn all you carnivores into vegetarians.

250g ready-made short crust pastry

2 tbsp olive oil

3 medium red onions – sliced

5 tbsp strawberry jam

1 - 2 tsp harissa paste

Oven: 190°C, 375°F, Gas Mark 5

SWEET ONION AND HARISSA JAM TARTS

If you're thinking that jam tarts seem a bit of a weird starter then you're wrong. These tarts are made with harissa, a hot fiery paste from North Africa, which is tamed by the strawberry jam. These tarts are ideal to serve with a barbecue as they can be eaten in fingers with drinks while the barbecuing is taking place.

Roll out pastry thinly on a lightly floured work surface. Using a round pastry cutter, 6cm (2 ½") in diameter, cut out as many circles as you can 20 - 24. Put into tart or muffin trays, prick the bottoms with a fork and cook in oven for 10 minutes.

Meanwhile, heat the olive oil in a saucepan. Add the sliced onions and cook gently over a low heat with the lid on for 10 minutes. Add jam and harissa and continue to cook for a further 5 minutes, stirring occasionally. Fill the tarts with the onion mixture and serve. If making in advance, allow onions and tarts to cool separately and refrigerate the onions and keep the tarts in an air-tight container.

◗ May be prepared up to this stage the day before.

Fill the tarts and either serve cold or warm.

To re-heat – put on a baking tray on top of the barbecue for a few minutes or put back in the oven for 10 minutes.

MARINATED HALLOUMI, APRICOT AND COURGETTE KEBABS

750g (1lb 10oz) Halloumi cheese –
cut into 24 chunks

3 medium courgettes – cut into 24 slices

2 yellow peppers – de-seeded and
cut into 24 chunks

24 cherry tomatoes

24 dried apricots (approx 200g)

MARINADE

4 tbsp olive oil

2 garlic cloves – crushed or chopped

juice 1 lemon

3 handfuls fresh herbs, e.g. mint,
thyme, oregano

salt and pepper

Halloumi is a Greek cheese, usually made with ewes milk. It doesn't have a particularly strong flavour, but once marinated and grilled, it soaks up all the flavours and takes on a new dimension. It is ideal for barbecuing as it is quite elastic, and doesn't crumble easily.

You will need 8 kebab sticks. Allowing 3 pieces of cheese and vegetables per kebab, thread on to the sticks alternating ingredients as you go. Mix all marinade ingredients together and pour over the kebabs. Leave to marinate for at least 30 minutes or as long as possible.

◐ May be prepared up to this stage the day before.

Cook on a pre-heated barbecue, turning and basting with the marinade for about 15 minutes or until cheese begins to brown.

CHARGRILLED PEPPER AND CHICK PEA SALAD

2 tins (420g each) chick peas – drained

8 tbsp French dressing

salt and pepper

2 green and 2 red peppers – de-seeded
and cut into thick slices

There's no better way to cook peppers than on a barbecue. The blackened, charred skin adds to the intensity of their flavour.

Mix chick peas, French dressing, salt and pepper together in a large salad bowl.

☼ May be prepared up to this stage earlier in the day.

Put peppers on the barbecue, skin side down for 10 minutes and toss together with other ingredients while still hot.

Cook's tip: The peppers may also be charred under a very hot grill, skin side up, for 10 minutes.

BULGUR WHEAT WITH CUCUMBER, CORIANDER AND PUMPKIN SEEDS

 A lovely nutty, crunchy salad.

300g (10oz) bulgur wheat
600ml (1pt) water
½ cucumber – chopped
100g (3½oz) pumpkin seeds
3 handfuls chopped coriander
4 tbsp olive oil
juice of 1 lemon
salt and pepper

Allow bulgur wheat to soak in water for 30 minutes by which time all the water should have been absorbed. Add all remaining ingredients and season generously.

✳ May be made earlier in the day.

TORTILLA PANCAKES WITH PISTACHIO, SULTANAS AND CARAMELISED ORANGE SAUCE

Tortillas are always associated with savoury things but there's no reason why they can't be eaten sweet. They make a wonderfully unusual alternative to traditional pancakes as you will see from this recipe.

3 oranges
100g (3½oz) pistachio nuts – shelled
3 handfuls sultanas
200g (7oz) Greek yoghurt
8 large wheat tortillas
2 tbsp brown sugar
425ml (¾pt) orange juice
large slug Cointreau (approx 4 tbsp) or other liqueur

Peel the oranges, slice and cut the slices in quarters. Reserve 1 orange for the sauce but mix the others with pistachios, sultanas and Greek yoghurt. Lay a tortilla flat, put some of the filling on top and roll up. Repeat with the other tortillas.

To make sauce – put brown sugar, orange juice, Cointreau and remaining orange in a saucepan and boil rapidly for 10 minutes to reduce.

✳ May be prepared earlier in the day.

To heat pancakes – put in a flame-proof dish or baking tin and put on top of barbecue to warm or put in oven: 190°C, 375°F, Gas Mark 5 for 10 - 15 minutes. The sauce may be served hot or cold.

ORDER OF PREPARATION IF MAKING IN ADVANCE:

The day before:
1. Make tarts.
2. Make kebabs and marinate.

Earlier on the day:
3. Prepare chick peas up to ✳
4. Make bulgur wheat salad.
5. Prepare tortillas up to ✳

In the evening:
6. Light the barbecue.
7. Re-heat tarts or serve cold.
8. Cook kebabs and peppers for salad.
9. Warm tortillas and sauce.

ORDER OF PREPARATION IN UNDER 90 MINUTES:

1. Make kebabs and leave to marinate. Cook as needed.
2. Make bulgur wheat salad.
3. Light barbecue.
4. Prepare tortillas and warm as needed.
5. Make tarts.
6. Prepare chick pea salad and put peppers on barbecue as needed.

BLACK THAI

♀ A nutty white.
Recommendation – Thomas Mitchell
Marsanne from Australia

*T*hai food has become so incredibly popular, probably because it's so varied and full of interesting flavours and textures. It combines a mixture of Chinese, Indian and a number of exotic flavours from other Oriental cuisines. If you've steered away from Thai cooking because you've been worried about all the ingredients you'll need and the last minute preparation, then your worries are over. This elegant menu (hence the name) is designed for minimal last minute attention as so much of it can be prepared in advance and won't need a shopping list of ingredients as long as your arm.

MINI SEAFOOD SPRING ROLLS WITH A SWEET CHILLI SAUCE

24 crab sticks
1 tbsp soy sauce
1 packet fresh filo pastry   or 12 sheets (measuring approx 30cm x 18cm / 12" x 7")
ground nut or sesame oil for brushing
6 tsp sesame seeds
200g (7oz) bean sprouts
8 tsp sweet chilli dipping sauce ("Sharwoods" recommended)
Oven: 180°C, 350°F, Gas Mark 4

Even before you read the list of ingredients for this recipe, let me warn you that I'm using crab sticks (also known as seafood and ocean sticks). An ingredient which might make the top chefs of this world throw their hands up in disgust. Well let me assure you they work brilliantly in this recipe, look great and taste perfect.

Mix the crab sticks with soy sauce. Pile 12 sheets of filo on top of each other and cut in half lengthways. Take one piece at a time and brush lightly with oil. Put a crab stick at the end and roll up (the ends will be open). Repeat with remaining crab sticks. Put on a greased baking tray and sprinkle sesame seeds on top.

◐ May be prepared the day before.

Put in oven for 12 minutes or until golden. Put a handful of bean sprouts on each plate, a teaspoon of chilli sauce in the middle and arrange the spring rolls (3 per person) on top

Cook's tip: The spring rolls are also ideal as canapés for a drinks party. They can be arranged on a large platter with the chilli dipping sauce in a small bowl in the middle.

BAKED THAI GREEN CHICKEN

8 chicken breasts with skin
2 tsp green Thai curry paste ("Barts" recommended)
1 tin (400ml) coconut milk
2 garlic cloves
1 tbsp soy sauce
1 tbsp sugar
1 lime – cut into ⅛ wedges
3 handfuls chopped coriander
salt and pepper
Oven: 190°C, 375°F, Gas Mark 5

These chicken breasts stay moist and succulent with all the flavours from the marinade in which they are cooked. They are also delicious cooked on a barbecue.

Make 3 or 4 diagonal cuts across the chicken breasts and mix with all other ingredients, including the lime wedges but excluding 1 handful of coriander which should be reserved for decoration. Leave to marinate for at least 30 minutes or as long as possible.

◗ May be prepared the day before.

Put chicken and marinade in an oven-proof serving dish or roasting tin, cover and cook in oven for 1 hour. Half way through cooking, baste and take the cover off. Serve with the marinade and remaining coriander sprinkled on top.

Cook's tip: If you are barbecuing the chicken, use some of the marinade to baste it with and put the remainder in a saucepan, boil for 10 minutes and serve with chicken.

ORIENTAL CRUNCH SALAD

1 tbsp ground nut or olive oil
100g (3½oz) "Doll" or "Instant" noodles – broken up into small pieces
50g (2oz) flaked almonds
1 Chinese cabbage – sliced
8 spring onions – sliced on the diagonal
DRESSING
8 tbsp sesame oil
2 tbsp wine vinegar
2 tsp brown sugar
2 tbsp soy sauce
salt and pepper

I always tell my husband that gossiping in the car park of my daughter's school is very beneficial. It definitely proved to be in this case as I gleaned this delicious recipe from there. It was one of many salads that was made for a parents' lunch and was the only one to completely disappear, leaving the others to go soggy. It seems strange to fry dry noodles but it works and the crunchy effect is sensational. Thank you Lesley for the great idea.

Heat the oil in a frying pan and fry the noodles and almonds over a gentle heat for about 5 minutes, stirring occasionally, until golden. Remove from pan and allow to cool. Mix dressing ingredients together.

◗ May be prepared up to this stage the day before.

Mix everything together.

Cook's tip: Be careful when frying the noodles and almonds as they can burn easily if cooked on too high a heat.

SEVEN SPICE RICE TIMBALES

400g (14oz) Thai or basmati rice
2 tsp Thai 7 spice seasoning – see Cook's tip

Making timbales is so easy and bound to impress. On the other hand, if you prefer, you can forget about the timbales and just serve the rice in a bowl.

Cook rice according to instructions on the packet. Drain if necessary and mix with 7 spices. Pack tightly into warmed timbales or ramekin dishes and turn out on to serving plates.

Cook's tip: Schwartz make a very good Thai 7 spice seasoning but if you have problems finding it you can mix it yourself with some or all of the following: chilli powder, ginger, coriander, cinnamon, cumin, garlic, salt and pepper.

TOFFEE FONDUE WITH EXOTIC FRUIT

Due to the great popularity of the chocolate and fruit fondue in my first book, I have been "begged" to come up with an alternative version. It is also a great way to get children to eat fruit.

Unwrap toffees if necessary, and put in a saucepan with cream. Heat gently, stirring occasionally, until toffees have melted (this will take about 10 minutes).

◑ May be prepared the day before.

Re-heat toffee fondue – either in saucepan or put in microwave on high for 2-3 minutes until piping hot.

To serve – put toffee fondue into 2 small serving bowls and place on 2 platters with fruit arranged round them. Give each person a fork or fondue stick to dip fruit into toffee fondue.

Cook's tips: Exotic dried fruit may also be used in addition to fresh fruit, e.g. dried mango, pineapple, pear. This sauce is also delicious served over ice cream.

250g (9oz) dairy toffees	
300ml (½pt) double cream	
Choice of 4 different types of exotic fruit, e.g.	
mango – peeled and cubed	
pawpaw – peeled and cubed	
pineapple – peeled and cubed	
2 star fruit – sliced	
4 kiwi fruit – peeled and sliced	
100g (3½oz) cape gooseberries	

ORDER OF PREPARATION IF MAKING IN ADVANCE:

The day before:
1. Make toffee fondue.
2. Make spring rolls up to ◑
3. Make Thai chicken up to ◑
4. Make crunch salad up to ◑

In the evening:
5. Cook chicken as necessary.
6. Prepare fruit for fondue.
7. Put spring rolls in oven as needed.
8. Cook rice.
9. Assemble salad.

ORDER OF PREPARATION IN UNDER 90 MINUTES:

1. Prepare chicken and put in oven as needed.
2. Make crunch salad up to ◑ and toss together before serving.
3. Make spring rolls and put in oven as needed.
4. Cook rice.
5. Make fondue.

GOOD COD – A Wheat and Gluten Free Feast

♀ *A crisp, fresh Italian white. Recommendation – Le Fredis Pinot Grigio from Italy*

Not that long ago, anyone who said they had a food allergy was classed as a fussy eater. It has now become recognised that more and more people have an intolerance to certain foods which, if eaten, can make them seriously ill. About 1 in 1,200 people in the UK suffer from coeliac disease – an intolerance to gluten, a protein found in wheat, rye, barley and possibly oats. I personally know people who suffer from coeliac disease and also have friends who find that wheat disagrees with them and this is why I have come up with this menu.

POLENTA AND PESTO PIZZAS WITH SUN-DRIED TOMATOES AND GORGONZOLA

850ml (1½pts) water
225g (8oz) polenta or 500g (1lb 2oz) fresh ready-to-use polenta
25g (1oz) butter or Olivio
3 tbsp pesto (see Cook's tip below)
½ jar (140g) sun-dried tomatoes
200g (7oz) gorgonzola
1 bag (100g) mixed salad leaves
4 tbsp ready-made Italian or French dressing
salt and pepper
Oven: 200°C, 400°F, Gas Mark 6

Polenta is pre-cooked corn or maize meal. It is available as a grain and sometimes available from larger supermarkets and specialist delis in a ready-to-use form. For real speed, use the ready-to-use type if you can find it but check first that it contains no wheat.

If using polenta grain, put the water in a saucepan and bring to the boil. Add polenta and simmer, stirring every now and then for 5 minutes. Add butter/Olivio, pesto and season generously and cook for a further 2 minutes. Grease a swiss roll tin and spread the polenta mixture into the tin. Leave to cool.

◑ May be prepared up to this stage the day before.

❋ May be frozen.

Cut polenta into 8 rectangles but leave in the tin. (If using the fresh polenta, it may be already cut into 8 pieces, if not, slice and spread the pesto on top.) Put sun-dried tomatoes and slices of gorgonzola on top. Put in oven for 15 minutes. Serve polenta pizzas with the salad leaves and dressing drizzled over the leaves.

Cook's tip: You can either use a jar of pesto but I prefer the fresh pesto that you can buy in cartons.

ROAST COD IN A PARMESAN CRUST WITH A RED PEPPER, CAPER AND BLACK OLIVE COMPOTE

8 pieces (175g/6oz) thick cod fillet – skinned
100g (3½oz) grated Parmesan (see Cook's tip)
salt and pepper
COMPOTE
2 tins or jars (400g each) red pimentos – drained and sliced
1 jar capers – drained or rinsed if in salt
1 small tin or jar black olives – drained
juice of ¼ lemon
1 tbsp olive oil
2 tsp sugar
salt and pepper
Oven: 200°C, 400°F, Gas Mark 6

Cod are large fish, some growing as long as 120cm (4') and weighing up to 45kg (100lbs). Because of their size, you can get thick fillets which stay moist and juicy when cooked. Cod goes well with robust flavours and the compote not only complements the taste of the fish but its colours contrast to the white sweet flesh of the cod.

To make compote, mix all compote ingredients together.

◗ May be prepared the day before.

Put the compote into a large roasting tin and lay the cod on top. Sprinkle the grated Parmesan on top of the cod and put in oven for 20 minutes.

Cook's tip: I recommend buying a chunk of Parmesan and freshly grate it as needed – it gives a much better flavour.

SWEET POTATO BAKE

1.5kg (3lbs 5oz) sweet potatoes
1 handful chopped parsley
salt and pepper
Oven: 200°C, 400°F, Gas Mark 6

Sweet potatoes have a natural, sweet oiliness to them so no extra butter, oil or liquid is needed in this recipe.

Grease a large, flattish, oven-proof serving dish. Scrub the potatoes well and cut into ½cm (¼") slices. Layer slices in the dish seasoning as you go. Cover with foil and cook in oven for 50 minutes.

✻ May be prepared up to this point earlier in the day.

To re-heat – put back in oven for 20 minutes.
Sprinkle with parsley and serve.

Cook's tip: Sweet potatoes, like ordinary potatoes, will discolour quickly. Once they have been sliced and layered, they should be cooked immediately.

FRENCH BEANS IN WALNUT OIL

1kg (2lbs 4oz) French Beans
3 tbsp walnut oil
salt and pepper

It's amazing how the beans soak up the flavour of the oil to give a wonderfully nutty taste.

Top and tail the beans and cook in boiling water for about 10 minutes or until tender. Drain, return to the pan and toss in walnut oil, salt and pepper.

✻ May be cooked earlier in the day.

To re-heat – put in a microwavable serving bowl, cover with cling-film and microwave on high for 5 minutes, tossing half way through.

Cook's tip: If you have any beans left over, add some balsamic vinegar and eat them cold as a bean salad.

CHOCOLATE AMARETTI CAKE WITH PRALINE ICE CREAM

Amaretti biscuits are ideal to use for people on wheat-free diets as they are made out of ground almonds. Check the packet first as some of them have added flour. As there is no flour in this cake, it won't rise much but will be incredibly rich and "gooey" so only a small portion is needed.

250g (9oz) amaretti biscuits – wheat-free

110g (4oz) butter

4 heaped tbsp cocoa

4 level tbsp caster sugar

4 eggs

icing sugar for dusting

1 tub (500g) praline or other nutty ice cream ("Haagen-Dazs, Pralines and Cream" recommended)

Oven: 180°C, 350°F, Gas Mark 4

Turn the ice cream out into a serving bowl. Grease a spring-form or loose bottomed cake tin approx. 24cm (9½") in diameter. Put all the other ingredients into a food processor until smooth. Put into cake tin and cook for 30 minutes. The cake may be served hot or cold – see serving instructions below. If making in advance or serving cold, leave to cool in the tin.

◖ May be prepared the day before.

✳ May be frozen.

To serve – slide a flat knife around with edge of the tin and remove the sides. If serving hot, put back in oven for 15 minutes to warm. Dust with icing sugar and serve with a scoop of ice cream.

ORDER OF PREPARATION IF MAKING IN ADVANCE:

The day before:
1. Make polenta bases if using polenta grain.
2. Make red pepper compote.
3. Make chocolate cake.

Earlier on the day:
4. Cook sweet potato bake.
5. Cook beans.

In the evening:
6. Finish off polenta pizzas and put in oven as needed.
7. Get fish ready and put in oven when needed.
8. Re-heat potatoes
9. Re-heat beans.
10. Put chocolate cake in oven if serving warm.

ORDER OF PREPARATION IN UNDER 90 MINUTES:

1. Make polenta pizzas.
2. Make sweet potatoes.
3. Make compote and prepare fish.
4. Prepare beans and cook as needed.
5. Make chocolate cake.

BEIJING BANQUET

♀ A crisp, fruity white.
Recommendation – Casa Lapostolle,
Sauvignon Blanc from Chile

*M*y husband and I recently went on a trip to Beijing and Hong Kong. It was fascinating and was inspiring for new recipe ideas. There were some very interesting items on the menus (well that's when I could read them, because most were in Chinese) and here are some that I thought of including in this book: Braised Sea Cucumber with Pork Sinew and Sea Moss, Spicy Duck Webs, Smoked Pork Trotter with Jelly Fish and Braised Ox Penis with Radish – though I've never been too keen on radish myself... I decided to settle for those with ingredients from my local supermarket!

NOODLE NESTS WITH CRAB AND SPRING ONIONS

ground nut or olive oil
1 packet (250g) thread egg noodles (you will only need two sheets out of the three)
2 dressed crabs or 3 tins (170g each) crab meat
6 spring onions – thinly sliced
1 tub (250g) fromage frais
juice ½ lemon
1 Chinese cabbage
6 tbsp ready-made dressing
Oven: 220°C, 425°F, Gas Mark 7

I recently learnt that authentic birds nest soup was made with the saliva of birds! You'll be pleased to learn that my nests just have noodles.

You will need 1 or 2 twelve hole muffin or tart trays, brushed with oil. Pour boiling water over noodles, leave to stand for 5 minutes and drain well. Put the noodles in the muffin tins (you will need 24 nests in total so if you only have one muffin tray you will have to make this in two batches) and press down with the back of a spoon. Brush top of noodle nests with oil and put in oven for 15 minutes. Take out of tins and allow to cool. Keep in an airtight container until ready to use.

Meanwhile, mix crab with spring onions (reserve some of the green part for decoration), fromage frais, lemon juice and season.

◑ May be prepared up to this stage the day before.

Fill noodle nests with crab mixture and sprinkle the reserved green spring onions on top. Shred the Chinese cabbage, toss in dressing and divide between 8 plates. Put the nests on top, allowing 3 per person.

FISH AND OYSTER MUSHROOM SPRING ROLLS WITH A BLACK BEAN SAUCE

1 packet fresh filo pastry (or 16 sheets)

sesame or ground nut oil

8 thick cod fillets each weighing approx 140g (5oz)

125g (4½oz) oyster mushrooms

1 jar (160g) black bean sauce – "Sharwoods" recommended

2 tbsp soy sauce

4 tbsp sesame seeds

salt and pepper

Oven: 190°C, 375°F, Gas Mark 5

As spring rolls are usually deep fried, this often puts people off making them. In this recipe, I bake them in the oven – much easier, no smell of frying fish and a lot healthier.

Slice mushrooms and mix with black bean and soy sauces. Wash and dry cod fillets and cut a slit in each one and open out like a book. Stuff the mushroom mixture inside, season and fold the flap back. To make the spring rolls: Lay 2 sheets of filo, one on top of the other. Lightly brush the top one with oil. Lay the fish at one end and roll up until you get to within about 5cm (2") of the end. Fold in the edges and brush with oil to seal. Continue to roll until you get to the end. Repeat until you have 8 rolls. Place on a greased baking tray, fold side down. Brush with oil and sprinkle sesame seeds on top.

❄ May be made up to this point earlier in the day.

Cook, uncovered in oven for 25 minutes.

Cook's tip: Don't worry if the juices ooze out – just serve the juices with the spring rolls.

COCONUT RICE

450g (1lb) long grain rice

1 tin (400ml) coconut milk

600ml (1pt) vegetable or fish stock made with boiling water and 1 stock cube

salt and pepper

A Chinese meal without rice would be unthinkable. Coconut is also popular with the Chinese and the two go brilliantly together – hence this recipe.

Put rice in a saucepan with coconut milk and stock and bring up to the boil. Simmer for 15 minutes or until liquid is absorbed and rice is tender. Season and serve.

Microwave method – put rice in a non-metallic bowl with coconut milk and stock. Cover with cling-film, leaving a gap for steam to escape, microwave on high for 15 minutes and season.

Cook's tip: If you are going to use the microwave method, cook the rice in a non-metallic serving bowl and serve rice directly from microwave.

CHINESE VEGETABLE AND PEANUT SALAD WITH A SWEET AND SOUR DRESSING

500g (1lb 2oz) broccoli – cut into florets and the stalks sliced thinly

1 bunch spring onions – thickly sliced on the diagonal

1 red pepper – de-seeded and sliced

250g (9oz) baby corn

Even though stir-frys are very popular in China, they are a nuisance to have to cook at the last minute. This recipe contains typical vegetables for a stir-fry but I have turned it into a salad for ease of preparation.

To make dressing – mix all dressing ingredients together. Plunge the broccoli into boiling water to blanch for 3 minutes. Drain and rinse in cold water.

◑ May be prepared up to this stage the day before.

150g (5oz) bean sprouts
100g (3oz) salted roast peanuts
DRESSING
6 tbsp sesame or ground nut oil
2 tbsp wine vinegar
2 tbsp soy sauce
1 tbsp runny honey
salt and pepper

Toss all ingredients together in a large salad bowl.

Cook's tip: All the vegetables may be prepared earlier in the day and kept in polythene bags.

CRISPY RICE CAKES WITH GINGER, PAWPAW AND KIWI FRUIT

Do you remember those delicious rice crispy cakes you used to eat as a child? Well, this is an exotic variation with the addition of ginger and tropical fruits – quite yummy.

85g (3oz) butter
2 heaped tbsp caster or granulated sugar
100g (3½oz) rice crispies
1 jar stem ginger in syrup
2 pawpaw
4 kiwi fruit
1 tub (500ml) mango or passion fruit sorbet (optional)

Melt butter and sugar in a large saucepan. Chop 6 pieces of ginger and add to melted butter. Take off the heat and gently stir in rice crispies. Put into paper cake cases and put in fridge for at least 30 minutes.

◑ May be made up to this point a day or two before and kept in fridge until ready to serve.

Peel pawpaw and kiwi fruit and slice. Mix with 6 tablespoons of syrup from the stem ginger.

☼ The fruit may be prepared earlier in the day.

Take rice crispy cakes out of paper cases and serve with fruit and sorbet if required.

Cook's tip: The quantity of rice crispies makes more than 8 cakes. Either you can offer your guests "seconds" or if you have any left over you will find they are very popular with children.

ORDER OF PREPARATION IF MAKING IN ADVANCE:

The day before:
1. Make noodle nests, crab mixture, and make dressing.
2. Prepare broccoli and dressing for salad.
3. Make crispy rice cakes.

Earlier on the day:
4. Make spring rolls.
5. Prepare fruit for pudding.

In the evening:
6. Assemble starter.
7. Cook spring rolls.
8. Cook rice.
9. Finish off salad.

ORDER OF PREPARATION IN UNDER 90 MINUTES:

1. Make noodle nests up to ◑ and assemble before serving.
2. Make pudding up to ☼ and assemble before serving.
3. Make spring rolls and cook as needed.
4. Make salad.
5. Cook rice.

DAIRY-FREE DUCK

Not only is this a wonderful menu for a dinner party, but it is also completely dairy free. So if you have any friends who cannot eat dairy produce and you've been putting off having them for dinner, you've got no excuse now.

PRAWNS WITH A BLOODY MARY SALSA

 A wonderful starter to cure a hang-over!

1kg (2lbs 4oz) cooked prawns in shells
SALSA
3 medium tomatoes – cut in ¼
3 celery sticks – cut in ¼
½ red onion – cut in ½
2 handfuls fresh chopped coriander
1 tbsp Worcester sauce
2 tbsp vodka
salt and pepper

Put all salsa ingredients in a food processor and pulse to mix but do not blend too much.

Serve prawns with salsa. May also be served with granary bread or rolls.

Cook's tip: You'll need to provide finger bowls as peeling prawns can be a bit messy.

DUCK LEGS WITH A CONFIT OF CARAMELISED ONION AND PEAR

I love the combination of duck with fruit. In this recipe I have cheated a bit by using tinned pears which I find have a slight perfumed taste and work even better than fresh pears. I find cooking a whole duck a pain as I hate having to carve it so I have used leg portions which are available from most supermarkets.

8 duck leg portions
2 tbsp olive oil
2 red onions – sliced
2 tbsp brown sugar
1 tin (800g) pears - drained and sliced
Oven: 220°C, 425°F, Gas Mark 7

Prick the skin of the duck with a fork and rub with salt. Place on a rack in a roasting tin and cook for 45 minutes.

To make confit, melt the olive oil in a saucepan, add the onions and sugar and cook over a gentle heat with the lid on for about 10 minutes, stirring occasionally. Add the pears and continue to cook for a further 10 minutes. Serve with the duck.

☼ The confit may be made earlier in the day.

To re-heat – put saucepan over a gentle heat for 5 minutes.

CELERIAC AND MUSTARD MASH

2 medium sized celeriac – peeled and cut in large chunks

2 medium potatoes – scrubbed and cut in large chunks

50g (2oz) "Olivio" or margarine

3 tsp wholegrain mustard

salt and pepper

Celeriac is a rather ugly looking vegetable and I often wonder if that's the reason why it's not more widely eaten in this country though it's very popular in France. Considering it has such an unattractive outward appearance, the taste inside is surprisingly pleasing to eat. It is delicious mashed and cooking it this way, it can be prepared in advance and re-heated.

Put celeriac and potato into boiling water and simmer for 20 minutes until soft. Drain, return to pan and add "Olivio" or margarine, mustard, salt and pepper and mash with a potato masher.

◗ May be made the day before.

❄ May be frozen.

To re-heat either put in microwave on high for 7 minutes or put in oven: 190°C, 375°F, Gas Mark 5 for 20 minutes.

Cook's tip: If you have any left over, add some stock to make it into soup – delicious.

ROAST NEW POTATOES WITH ORANGE AND THYME

1.5kg (3lbs 5oz) new potatoes – scrubbed

3 tbsp olive oil

zest and juice of 1 orange

1 handful chopped thyme

2 garlic cloves – chopped or crushed

salt and pepper

Oven: 220°C, 425°F, Gas Mark 7

Roast potatoes are always popular, but new potatoes roasted are even more popular, so don't expect any left-overs.

Put all ingredients into a roasting tin and cook in oven for 1 hour tossing occasionally.

Cook's tip: This recipe works equally well using large potatoes cut into cubes.

FILO BASKETS WITH BLACKBERRIES, CASSIS AND BLACKCURRANT SORBET

oil for greasing

1 packet fresh filo or 16 sheets (measuring approx 30cm x 18cm/ 12" x 7")

1 litre blackcurrant sorbet

300g (10½oz) blackberries or other berries (see Cook's tip below)

large slug of cassis (approx 4 tbsp)

icing sugar for dusting

Oven: 180°C, 350°F, Gas Mark 4

If you have a copy of my first book, you will realise that I'm very keen on filo baskets, parcels, etc. They have proved to be very popular as they are much easier to make than you think, can be made in advance and look incredibly impressive. In this recipe, I am only using oil to grease the bowls which are going to be used as moulds, but not using oil to brush between the sheets. This will save time and give a really light effect. If you are in a real rush, and haven't got time to make the filo baskets, just serve the sorbet and fruit with dairy-free biscuits or, in the case of people who eat dairy products, ready-made brandysnap baskets.

To make the filo baskets you will need oven-proof bowls to mould the pastry in (about 11cm/4" in diameter).

Brush the insides of the bowls with oil to stop the filo sticking. Take one sheet and fold in half to form a square. Take a second sheet, fold it in half as well and lay it on top of the other at an angle to form an 8 pointed star. Place inside the bowl and repeat 7 more times. (If you do not have 8 bowls, they can be done in batches.) Cook in oven for 10 minutes and leave to cool.

◑ May be made the day before.

❋ May be frozen.

Mix the blackberries with cassis. Fill each filo basket with two scoops of sorbet and blackberries with cassis. Dust generously with icing sugar.

Cook's tips: If blackberries aren't in season, other fruit may be used instead, e.g. raspberries, strawberries, fresh or frozen.

ORDER OF PREPARATION IF MAKING IN ADVANCE:

The day before:
1. Make celeriac mash.
2. Make filo baskets.

Earlier on the day:
3. Make bloody mary salsa.
5. Make pear confit.

In the evening:
6. Prepare and roast potatoes as necessary.
7. Cook duck.
8. Re-heat celeriac and pear confit.
9. Mix blackberries with cassis and assemble just before serving.

ORDER OF PREPARATION IN UNDER 90 MINUTES:

1. Make filo baskets and mix blackberries with cassis.
2. Prepare and roast potatoes as necessary.
3. Prepare duck and confit and cook as necessary.
4. Prepare celeriac and cook as necessary.
5. Make bloody mary salsa.

Opposite: Dairy-Free Duck (page 94)

OLD FAVOURITES

♀ *A full flavoured white.
Recommendation – Wolf Blass Barrel
Fermented Chardonnay from
Australia*

*P*eople are always drooling over the type of food they ate as children –
spotted dick, jam roly-poly, macaroni cheese, fish pie and many
others. This whole menu is compiled from real old fashioned "comfort"
food but with a stylish twist to make it trendy by today's standards and
smart enough for a dinner party.

EGG MAYONNAISE WITH ANCHOVIES AND SUN-DRIED TOMATOES ON CROUTONS

8 thick slices granary or wholemeal bread
25g (1oz) butter
8 eggs – hard boiled
8 tbsp mayonnaise
1 tin anchovies – drained
½ jur sun-dried tomatoes in oil – slice tomatoes and reserve 4 tbsp of the oil from the jar
1 bag (150g) mixed salad leaves
2 tbsp balsamic vinegar
salt and pepper
Oven: 200°C, 400°F, Gas Mark 6

Have you ever been to a children's tea party and found that all the egg mayonnaise sandwiches have been scoffed by the adults before the children can even say abracadabra? Well, I've seen that happen so many times that I thought it was about time I came up with a sophisticated version of egg mayonnaise so that adults can enjoy it in their own right.

Using a cup or saucer as a guide, cut a circle out of each slice of bread, as large as possible but avoiding the crusts (reserve outer bits for the treacle tart) Spread one side of each circle with butter and place on a baking tray, butter side up. Put in oven for 10 minutes.

◑ The croutons may be made in advance and kept in an air-tight container for up to 3 days.

To assemble – put one crouton on the centre of each plate and arrange the leaves around the outside. Slice the hard boiled eggs and place, fanned out, on top of each crouton topped with a blob of mayonnaise. Arranged sun-dried tomatoes and anchovies on top and season. Mix the 4 tbsp oil from the sun-dried tomatoes with the balsamic vinegar and drizzle over the leaves.

Opposite: Old Favourites (page 97)

SCALLOP, PRAWN, MUSSEL, SMOKED COD AND SPINACH PIE TOPPED WITH GRUYÈRE RÖSTI

500g (1lb 2oz) frozen leaf spinach – de-frosted and drained

400g (14oz) mixed uncooked seafood (see Cook's tip below) – de-frosted if frozen

450g (1lb) cod fillet – skinned and cut into chunks

350g (12oz) smoked cod fillet – skinned and cut into chunks

1 tub (300g – 350g) fresh cheese sauce

2 long life packets (400g each) rösti

110g (4oz) Gruyère – grated

175g (6oz) cooked prawns in shells (optional)

pepper and paprika

Oven: 220°C, 425°F, Gas Mark 7

A really luxurious fish pie using a mixture of shellfish, smoked and unsmoked cod and topped with rösti oozing with Gruyère. It looks extremely impressive served in individual bowls or can be put in one or two large gratin type dishes.

Mix spinach, all fish, except prawns in shells, and cheese sauce together and season with pepper. Put into individual bowls or large gratin dish(es). Mix rösti with grated Gruyère and spread on top of the fish mixture.

☀ May be prepared up to this stage earlier in the day.

Put in oven, uncovered, for 25 minutes if in individual bowls or 35 minutes for a larger dish. 10 minutes before the end of cooking, place the prawns in shells on top of the rösti and sprinkle with paprika.

Cook's tips: Most large supermarkets sell either fresh or frozen uncooked mixed seafood. It usually contains a mixture of prawns, mussels, squid and scallops. If you cannot find this, then buy a mixture of the seafood separately. Don't add extra salt as the smoked cod and rösti are both quite salty.

BEETROOT WITH MARMALADE

1kg (2lbs 4oz) natural cooked beetroot – drained and sliced

2 tbsp marmalade

I'm always surprised that beetroot is so rarely served as a vegetable. I love the vibrant colour and the addition of marmalade adds a wonderful sweetness. If you have enough room in the oven, it can be baked, if not, cook it in a saucepan.

Either put beetroot in an oven-proof serving dish and spoon marmalade on top. Cover with foil and put in oven for 30 minutes or put in saucepan, cover with lid and cook gently for 15 minutes, stirring occasionally.

TREACLE, KUMQUAT AND GINGER TART

 This is such a lovely sweet sticky tart but can tend to be a bit too sickly. I have added kumquats to liven it up and give more tartness.

250g (9oz) ready-made short-crust pastry

8 heaped tbsp golden syrup

8 heaped tbsp breadcrumbs – made from left-overs from croutons – (see Cook's tip below)

2 tsp ground ginger

12 kumquats – sliced

zest and juice of ½ lemon

Oven: 200°C, 400°F, Gas Mark 6

Roll out pastry and line a tart or flan tin, preferably loose-bottomed, about 28cm (11") in diameter. Put in fridge while preparing filling. Put golden syrup in a saucepan over a low heat until runny. Add breadcrumbs and leave for 10 minutes to soak in. (At this stage the mixture should have the consistency of thick honey, add more breadcrumbs if too runny or more syrup if too stodgy.) Add ginger, kumquats, zest and lemon juice and put into pastry case. Put in oven for 30 minutes.

◖ May be made the day before.

❋ May be frozen.

May be served hot or cold with Greek yoghurt, fromage frais or ice cream. To re-heat – put back in oven: 180°C, 350°F, Gas Mark 4 for 15 minutes.

Cook's tip: To make breadcrumbs – put crusts and bits into a food processor until crumbs are formed. Any extra breadcrumbs can be frozen and used as needed. To make it easier to measure the golden syrup, heat spoon in boiling water first.

ORDER OF PREPARATION IF MAKING IN ADVANCE:

The day before:
1 Make croutons and hard boil eggs.
2. Make treacle tart.

Earlier on the day:
3. Prepare fish pie up to ❋

In the evening:
4. Prepare beetroot and cook as needed.
5. Cook fish pie as needed.
6. Assemble starter.
7. Re-heat treacle tart.

ORDER OF PREPARATION IN UNDER 90 MINUTES:

1. Make croutons and hard boil eggs.
2. Prepare fish pie and cook as needed.
3. Prepare beetroot and cook as needed.
4. Prepare treacle tart and put in oven 30 minutes before needed.

DINNER IN HALF THE TIME

*♀ A soft, fruity red.
Recommendation – Redwood Trail
Pinot Noir from California*

I have given this menu the above title because it's so incredibly quick that it can be done in a flash – to be precise – 45 minutes.

500g (1lb 2oz) frozen chopped spinach
250g (9oz) frozen sweet corn
1 tin (400ml) coconut milk
2 tbsp soy sauce
2 chicken stock cubes
1.3 litres (2¼pts) boiling water
4 tsp "Bart's" ready prepared lemon grass or 2 stalks lemon grass finely chopped
2 tsp red Thai curry paste – "Bart's" recommended (optional)
200g (7oz) prawns (may be frozen and de-frosted)
1 handful fresh coriander – chopped
salt and pepper

SPINACH, PRAWN AND LEMON GRASS SOUP

 This is a lovely aromatic soup which can be made in minutes. There is no need to de-frost the spinach or sweet corn.

Throw all ingredients except prawns and coriander into a saucepan. Bring up to boil and simmer for a couple of minutes then add prawns. Serve with coriander sprinkled on top.

Cook's tips: The red Thai curry paste will give this soup a real buzz but be cautious as it's very fiery. The soup may be served with prawn crackers, prawn toasts or poppadoms.

8 duck breasts
5 tbsp ginger conserve
1 jar (160g) black bean sauce
300ml (½pt) orange juice
Oven: 230°C, 450°F, Gas Mark 8

DUCK WITH GINGER, ORANGE AND BLACK BEAN SAUCE

 I love duck with oriental flavours and have used duck breasts for ease and speed. Cutting slits in the skin and rubbing salt in helps to crisp it up.

Cut three diagonal slits in the skin of the duck and rub with salt. Put the ginger conserve, black bean sauce and orange juice in a saucepan.

☀ May be prepared earlier in the day.

Put duck on a rack over a roasting dish and cook for 30 minutes. Reserve 3 tbsp of the sauce to brush over the duck half way through cooking. Bring the remainder of the sauce up to the boil and allow to simmer for about 10 minutes.

To serve – thinly slice the duck breasts and fan out on individual plates. Pour the sauce on top.

Cook's tip: The duck breasts look very impressive when they are sliced and fanned out but if you find this too much to do, just serve them whole with the sauce on top.

ORIENTAL SESAME VEGETABLES WITH NOODLES

400g (14oz) baby carrots

400g (14oz) dwarf courgettes

250g (9oz) French beans –
topped and tailed

250g (9oz) baby corn

2 packets (250g/9oz) medium
egg noodles

3 tbsp sesame oil

4 tbsp sesame seeds

salt and pepper

I have used baby vegetables in this recipe as they need very little preparation – just a quick wash. They are cooked together with the noodles to save washing up!

Cook vegetables in a very large saucepan in boiling water for around 5 minutes. Add the noodles, and simmer for a further 3 minutes. Drain well and toss in sesame oil, sesame seeds, salt and pepper.

Cook's tip: Normal sized carrots and courgettes may be used but you will need to slice them or cut them into batons.

HOT SPICED RICE PUDDING WITH LYCHEES AND MANGO

1 large tin (850g) rice pudding

1 tin (425g) lychees – drained
and cut in half

1 tin (425g) mango – drained
and chopped

2-3 tsp allspice or cinnamon

4 tbsp brown sugar

Oven: 290°C, 375°F, Gas Mark 5

Delicious warming comfort food with an oriental slant. You can use fresh mango and lychees but for real speed I prefer to use tinned fruit and, as it is cooked, the difference is very slight. This pudding looks good cooked in ramekin dishes or small oven-proof bowls but can also be cooked in one large dish.

Mix together rice pudding, lychees, mango and allspice/cinnamon. Either put in 8 ramekin dishes or one flattish oven-proof serving dish. Sprinkle the sugar on top.

❄ May be prepared earlier in the day.

Put in oven for 20 minutes if in ramekins and 25 minutes if in one big dish until sugar starts to bubble on top.

ORDER OF PREPARATION IF MAKING
IN ADVANCE:

Earlier in the day:
1. Prepare duck up to ❄
2. Prepare rice pudding up to ❄
3. Wash and prepare vegetables – keep in a polythene bag until ready to use.

In the evening:
4. Cook duck.
5. Make soup.
6. Cook vegetables and noodles.
7. Put rice pudding in oven as necessary.

ORDER OF PREPARATION IN
UNDER 45 MINUTES:

1. Prepare and cook duck recipe.
2. Prepare rice pudding and put in oven as needed.
3. Prepare vegetables and noodles and cook as needed.
4. Make soup.

NO FUSS FRENCH

2 jars (800ml each) fish soup –
"Select Marée" or Waitrose own brand
recommended

1kg (2lbs 4oz) fresh mussels in shells

French bread

The French produce some of the best food in the world and they are incredibly particular about eating well. They are also fussy about the way they cook, taking hours over making sauces, stocks and soups. The finished results are usually delicious but I think you'll find my short-cut methods taste just as good.

MUSSEL SOUP

Mussel soup always reminds me of the first time we went to France with our twins who were three at the time. The hotel we were staying in said they could provide a special childrens' menu and on the first night, the children were given mussel soup – well, I was delighted because I ate it myself. I was quite relieved that I'd brought a jar of Marmite with me so that I could make marmite sandwiches! Obviously three year old French children must have more sophisticated taste than three year old English children.

Prepare the mussels by scrubbing them under cold running water and pulling off the beard (hairy bit). Heat the soup in a very large saucepan until boiling, add mussels and simmer for about 7 minutes or until the mussels open. Serve with warm crusty French bread – see Handy Hints page 11.

Cook's tip: There are many different theories about storing mussels. The best solution is to buy them on the day you are going to eat them and just keep them refrigerated. If you want to buy them the day before, I was always told to keep them in water with flour or oatmeal which is meant to feed them. I have since heard that they can die from drowning. The new theory is that you should wrap them in damp newspaper (preferably Le Monde!) and keep them in a cool place. After cleaning them, if any remain open, discard them because they are dead, likewise, if any do not open once cooked.

ROAST POUSSIN WITH LEMON, GARLIC AND TARRAGON

4 poussin – cut in half

3 lemons – zest and juice

3 tbsp olive oil

6 garlic cloves – crushed

4 handfuls fresh tarragon – chopped

1 tub (200ml) crème fraîche – the half
fat type may be used

salt and pepper

Oven: 200°C, 400°F, Gas Mark 6

Tarragon is one of the most important herbs in the French kitchen so I am using loads of it in this recipe. I have allowed half a poussin per person, but if you have guests with large appetites, allow a whole one each. In this recipe I have simply roasted them with masses of garlic, lemon and tarragon to give a real French flavour.

Mix the zest and juice of the lemons, olive oil, crushed garlic, chopped tarragon, salt and pepper together and pour over the poussin. Leave to marinate for 30 minutes or preferably longer if possible.

◐ May be prepared up to this stage the day before.

Put poussin and marinade in a roasting dish and cook in oven for 1 hour, basting occasionally.

Once cooked, transfer the poussin to a serving plate, put the roasting dish with all the juices over a low heat and add crème fraîche. Stir to amalgamate and serve with poussin.

Cook's tip: If you prefer, chicken breasts or portions may be used instead.

ROAST VEGETABLE RATATOUILLE

I love roast vegetables and I love ratatouille, so the two combined has turned out to be one of my favourite recipes. Roasting the vegetables first, helps to retain the colour and shape.

1 red, 1 yellow and 1 green pepper – de-seeded and cut into thick slices

2 red onions – cut into eighths

6 courgettes – preferably yellow but the green ones will do – thickly sliced

1 large or 2 small aubergines – sliced

2 garlic cloves – sliced

3 tbsp olive oil

1 tin (400g) chopped tomatoes

salt and pepper

Oven: 200°C, 400°F, Gas Mark 6

Put all ingredients except the tinned tomatoes in a large roasting dish. Put in oven for 50 minutes, tossing occasionally. Add tinned tomatoes and put back in oven for another 10 minutes.

◑ May be prepared the day before.

❋ May be frozen.

To re-heat – either put in microwave on high for 8 minutes, stirring half way through or re-heat gently in a saucepan for approx. 12 minutes.

Cook's tip: This is also delicious served cold as a salad with the addition of 2 tbsp balsamic vinegar.

GRATIN OF NEW POTATOES WITH RACLETTE

Raclette is actually a Swiss cheese but is also popular in France. It is often melted over an open fire or purpose-made raclette heater, scraped off as it melts and eaten with potatoes.

1.5kg (3lbs 5oz) new potatoes

250g (9oz) raclette or other French cheese – (see Cook's tip below)

Plunge potatoes into salted, boiling water and allow to simmer for about 10 minutes or until potatoes are tender but still have a bit of crunch. Drain and put in a flattish oven-proof serving dish or gratin dish. Slice the cheese and lay slices on top. If serving immediately put under grill for 2-3 minutes until cheese is melted and bubbling.

❋ May be prepared earlier in the day.

To re-heat – put in oven: 200°C, 400°F, Gas Mark 6 for 20 minutes.

Cook's tip: Other suitable cheese to use is Reblochon, Saint-Paulin, Tomme de Savoie (hard or soft), Camembert or Brie.

CRÊPES WITH APPLES AND RAISINS IN CALVADOS

8 ready-made crêpes

25g (1oz) butter

*700g (1lb 9oz) apple purée –
sold in jars or tins*

2 eating apples – peeled and chopped

2 handfuls raisins

3 tbsp brown sugar

*very large slug Calvados – at least
4 tbsp or as much as you dare*

Oven: 190°C, 375°F, Gas Mark 5

There's nothing better than a good crêpe but I find them a real bore to make as the cook has to spend a long time standing over a frying pan cooking them individually. By the time you've finished cooking them, they've all been eaten and there aren't any left for you. Well, I suppose it's good for the diet! You've probably guessed by now that my recipe doesn't involve standing over a frying pan for a long time, but buying the crêpe ready-made. I am so pleased that they are now available from major supermarkets and that they are delicious, especially with the addition of this wonderful stuffing and Calvados.

Grease a large gratin or flattish oven-proof serving dish with half the butter. Mix the apple purée, chopped apples, raisins and 2 tbsp brown sugar together. Divide the filling between the eight crêpes, roll the filling up inside and put into the greased dish. Smear the remaining butter and 1 tbsp sugar over the top and cover with foil.

☀ May be prepared up to this stage earlier in the day.

Put in oven for 20 minutes. Pour Calvados over the crêpes and serve. May be served with crème fraîche, fromage frais or ice cream.

Cook's tip: Brandy or Cointreau may be used instead of Calvados.

ORDER OF PREPARATION IF MAKING IN ADVANCE:

The day before:
1. Make ratatouille.
2. Marinate the poussin.

Earlier on the day:
3. Make potatoes up to ☀
4. Make crêpes up to ☀
5. Clean the mussels.

In the evening:
6. Cook poussin as needed.
7. Re-heat ratatouille and potatoes as necessary.
8. Make soup.
9. Put crêpes in oven when necessary.

ORDER OF PREPARATION IN UNDER 90 MINUTES:

1. Marinate poussin and cook as needed.
2. Make ratatouille
3. Prepare crêpes and put in oven 30 minutes before needed.
4. Cook potatoes.
5. Make soup.

CONTEMPORARY ITALIAN

*T*his Italian menu has a bit of French influence creeping in by including a soufflé as the starter. Even though traditionally French, this soufflé is made with Italian cheese and is unconventional in the method of cooking as it can be made in advance. If you've always steered clear of soufflés now is your chance so find out how to cook them with confidence.

SPINACH AND DOLCELATTE SOUFFLÉ

oil for greasing

250g (9oz) frozen leaf spinach – de-frosted

175g (6oz) dolcelatte – grated

200ml crème fraîche – the half fat type may be used

5 eggs

salt and pepper

Oven: 190°C, 375°F, Gas Mark 5

The most amazing thing about this soufflé is that you can make it in advance and keep it in the freezer until you need it. It's cooked from frozen so you'll have no last minute panic whisking egg white when you'd rather be drinking with your guests.

Brush 8 ramekin dishes with oil. Mix the spinach, dolcelatte, crème fraîche and egg yolks together. Whisk the whites until stiff and fold into the spinach mixture. Pour into the ramekins and either cook immediately or put in the freezer uncooked.

❄ May be kept in the freezer for up to 2 months.

If cooking immediately, put in oven for 20 minutes. If cooking from the freezer, put in oven frozen and cook for 30 minutes. Serve with warm Italian bread, e.g. ciabatta or focaccia – see Handy Hints page 11.

Cook's tip: Dolcelatte is quite creamy and can disintegrate when grated – don't worry if this happens, just crumble it.

PORK PIZZAIOLA WITH PEPPERONI

8 pork escalopes

1 jar (420g) pasta sauce –
see Cook's tip

150g (5oz) pepperoni- thinly sliced

1 small tin or jar black olives (optional)

2 handfuls basil

salt and pepper

Oven: 190°C, 375°F, Gas Mark 5

Pizzaiola sauce originates from Naples and is similar to the type of sauce used when making pizzas. Pepperoni, which is a spicy, dry Italian sausage, is also often served with pizzas so goes ideally with this dish to give it a spicy touch.

Place pork escalopes in one layer in a large oven-proof serving dish (you may need to use two). Pour the pasta sauce on top, and then add sliced pepperoni, black olives and one handful of basil, shredded. Season and cover with foil.

◑ May be prepared up to this stage the day before.

Put in oven for 30 minutes but no longer as the pork tends to become tough if over cooked. Serve decorated with the remaining basil.

Cook's tips: Any type of ready-made pasta sauce may be used but I especially like "Waitrose Pasta sauce with Garlic" or "Loyd Grossman's Sweet Red Pepper Sauce". This recipe can be made using turkey or veal escalopes instead of pork and the pepperoni may be substituted by chorizo. If you don't like spicy food, then halve the quantity of pepperoni or chorizo.

GNOCCHI WITH PESTO

500g (1lb 2oz) gnocchi

½ tub (90g) pesto - preferably fresh

These small Italian dumplings, made from potato, flour or polenta, are now readily available from most supermarkets or delis, sold either fresh or in sealed long-life packages.

Cook gnocchi as instructions on packet. Drain and toss in pesto.

BALSAMIC BROCCOLI

1.3kg (3lbs) broccoli

3 tbsp balsamic vinegar

salt and pepper

Balsamic vinegar is often used in dressings for salads, but it is also delicious tossed together with hot vegetables. A small amount of this dark, sweet-sour vinegar goes a long way and gives the broccoli a unique mellow flavour.

Cut the thick stalks off the broccoli and break up into florets. Add to boiling water and cook for 7 minutes. Drain well and toss in balsamic vinegar, salt and pepper.

Cook's tip: Balsamic vinegars range in price quite dramatically. There is no need to have to take out a loan from the bank to buy a bottle, just buy one of the more moderately priced ones and it will still have a wonderful effect.

PASSION FRUIT AND MARSHMALLOW SEDUCTION

300g (10 ½oz) digestive biscuits

85g (3oz) butter

8 passion fruit

1 (200g) packet marshmallows

300ml (½pt) double cream

 The name speaks for itself – this is a kind of tart that's tempting, alluring, enticing and could lead you astray!

You will need a tart tin, preferably loose bottomed (28cm/11" in diameter). Crush biscuits, melt butter and mix together. Put into tart tin and push down and up the sides with the back of a spoon. Put in fridge while preparing the filling. Scoop out the pulp of 4 passion fruit, put into a saucepan and add marshmallows. Heat gently until marshmallows have melted and allow to cool slightly. Whisk cream until thick and fold marshmallow mixture into the cream. Spread on top of biscuit base and put back in fridge to chill for at least 1 hour.

◗ May be made the day before.

❋ May be frozen.

To serve – remove sides of tin and put tart on a serving plate. Cut remaining 4 passion fruit in half. Slice tart and serve each portion with half a passion fruit.

ORDER OF PREPARATION IF MAKING IN ADVANCE:

The day before:
1. Make soufflé and put in freezer.
2. Prepare pork pizzaiola up to ◗
3. Make chocolate seduction.

In the evening:
4. Put soufflés in oven as needed.
5. Put pork in oven as needed.
6. Cook broccoli and gnocchi.

ORDER OF PREPARATION IN UNDER 90 MINUTES:

1. Make chocolate seduction.
2. Prepare pork and put in oven as needed.
3. Prepare soufflés and put in freezer until needed to cook.
4. Cook broccoli and gnocchi.

JAPAN IN A DASHI

♀ An oaky Semillon.
Recommendation – Peter Lehmann
Semillon from Australia

*H*ave you always thought that Japanese cooking was totally out of the question – all those weird ingredients that you have to go half way to Tokyo to buy and all the days of preparation. Well, read on and find out how I have made Japanese cooking easy and accessible. These days most large supermarkets sell some Japanese staples, such as seaweed, sushi or sticky rice and other traditional fare. By the way, dashi is a Japanese stock made out of seaweed and fish.

On the subject of drinks, traditionally, green tea or sake (made from fermented rice and served hot or cold) is drunk with a meal, however, you may prefer to drink a nice cold beer, or in my case, a nice cold wine.

SUBURBAN SUSHI

450g (1lb) sushi rice or
Thai fragrant rice
750ml (1¼pts) water
3 tbsp rice vinegar
1 tbsp sugar
1 tsp salt
6 sheets nori seaweed
9 crab/seafood sticks
9 baby corn
Japanese Soy Sauce
100g (3½oz) pickled ginger (optional)
wasabi paste, Japanese horseradish (optional)

Sushi is now becoming very popular in this country with sushi bars opening up everywhere. Quite often the food is moved around on a conveyor belt for customers to help themselves. Seaweed plays a major role in Japanese cuisine and around 300,000 tonnes of it are consumed every year. As this is a major ingredient of sushi and now more easily available, I have used nori seaweed in this recipe. Raw fish is also often used but as it is not always popular with our Western palate and also has to be eaten extremely fresh, I'm not using it.

Put rice in a saucepan with the water, bring up to the boil and simmer for about 10 minutes or until all water has been absorbed. Stir in rice vinegar, sugar and salt, cover and leave to cool.

Lay one sheet of seaweed on a piece of kitchen towel or a sushi mat with the widest part towards you. Spread ⅙ of the rice over the seaweed leaving about 2.5cm (1") uncovered at the far end. Lay 3 of the crab sticks in a line across the middle of the rice and damp the edge of the uncovered bit of seaweed with water as this will help it stick better. Use the towel to help you roll the seaweed round the filling tightly. Repeat this process with the remaining crab sticks and with the baby corn until you have used up the 6 sheets of seaweed and have 6 rolls. Leave to chill for at least 10 minutes.

◑ May be made up to this point the day before.

Cut each roll into 6 slices (allowing 4 slices per person) and serve with some soy sauce for dipping. Pickled ginger and wasabi may also be served with the sushi.

Cook's tip: A good way of serving the soy sauce is to cut a cucumber into 4cm (1½") chunks, using a melon baller, hollow out part of the middle, and put the soy sauce inside.

TERIYAKI SALMON WITH WATER CHESTNUTS

*8 portions skinned salmon fillet –
175g (6oz) each or 1.3kg (3lbs) in total*

1 tin (220g) water chestnuts – drained

8 tbsp teriyaki marinade

Along with rice, fish is one of Japan's staple foods eaten almost daily. Tokyo has the largest fish market in the world, selling up to 150 different types of fish. There are many varieties of unusual fish that I could use for this recipe but I have decided that salmon goes as well as any for colour and taste.

Mix salmon with the water chestnuts and teriyaki marinade. Leave to marinate for at least 30 minutes.

◗ May be prepared the day before.

Cook over roast vegetables – see recipe below.

ROAST JAPANESE VEGETABLES WITH GINGER

*500g (1lb 2oz) carrots – peeled
and cut into batons*

*400g (14oz) French beans –
topped and tailed*

250g (9oz) baby corn

*16 spring onions – cut in ½ on
the diagonal*

*175g (6oz) lotus root (optional) –
peeled and sliced*

*3cm (1¼") cube fresh ginger –
peeled and chopped*

*2 handfuls of either chopped coriander
or mint or both*

4 tbsp ground nut or olive oil

salt and pepper

Oven: 220°C, 425°F, Gas Mark 7

Traditionally, the Japanese steam, boil, stir-fry or pickle their vegetables. I have chosen to be a bit of a rebel and roast my vegetables for ease. Not only can they be cooked together with the salmon but they taste quite delectable in this manner.

Prepare the vegetables.

◗ The vegetables may be prepared the day before and stored in a sealed polythene bag in the fridge.

Put all ingredients in a very large roasting tin or two medium sized ones. Put in oven for 15 minutes, then lay the salmon on top in one layer and pour over the marinade. Roast in oven for a further 15 minutes.

To serve – place the rice noodles (see following recipe) on each serving plate with the salmon on top. The vegetables may be piled on top of the salmon or served separately.

RICE NOODLES WITH SESAME OIL

500g (1lb 2oz) flat rice noodles or medium egg noodles

3 tbsp sesame oil or olive oil

3 tbsp Japanese soy sauce

salt and pepper

In this recipe, I have used flat rice noodles, sometimes referred to as "rice sticks". Do not use the very thin rice noodles for stir-frying as they will not work done this way. If you can't find flat rice noodles, then use medium egg noodles instead.

Cook noodles as instructions on packet. Drain and toss in oil, soy sauce and season.

EXOTIC STICKY FRUIT PANCAKES

1 small tin (200g) condensed milk

142ml (¼pt) double cream

4 passion fruit – cut in half and flesh scooped out

4 kiwi – peeled, sliced and cut in half

1 medium mango – peeled and cut into chunks (or 1 tin (400g) mangoes drained and cut in chunks)

1 tin (400g) lychees – drained

16 cape gooseberries (physalis)

8 scotch pancakes with raisins

8 tsp ginger wine

icing sugar for dusting

The Japanese tend to eat fresh fruit for dessert but thick pancakes are also popular and condensed milk is sometimes used. I have used a combination of them all and, though I say so myself, it's quite delicious.

Mix together condensed milk, cream, passion fruit, kiwi, mango and lychees.

◗ May be prepared up to this stage the day before.

Put one pancake on each plate and pour over the ginger wine. Pile the fruit mixture on top and decorate with the cape gooseberries. Dust with icing sugar.

Cook's tip: Other fruit may be used instead, for example, pawpaw, banana, melon.

ORDER OF PREPARATION IF MAKING IN ADVANCE:

The day before:
1. Make sushi.
2. Marinate salmon.
3. Prepare vegetables.
4. Prepare pudding up to ◗

In the evening:
5. Slice sushi.
6. Put vegetables and salmon in oven as needed.
7. Cook noodles.
8. Assemble pancakes before serving.

ORDER OF PREPARATION IN UNDER 90 MINUTES:

1. Make sushi.
2. Marinate salmon.
3. Prepare vegetables and cook with salmon as needed.
4. Prepare sticky fruit pancakes.
5. Cook noodles.

PLEASURES OF PROVENCE

♀ *A spicy, fruity red.*
Recommendation – James Herrick
Cuvée Simone from France

*L*ast summer my husband Nick, twins Jack and Katie and I went to Provence for a holiday. Together with our friends, The Bottings, we rented a lovely, secluded converted farm house with a swimming pool. We had a wonderful holiday, lazing by the pool during the day and testing out the local food and wine in the evening (all part of the onerous work of being a cookery writer). The following recipes were inspired by the local produce.

SALAD OF ENDIVE, LARDONS AND BRIOCHE CROUTONS WITH A WARM GOATS CHEESE DRESSING

6tbsp olive oil
225g (8oz) lardons or diced streaky bacon
4 brioche or 1 small loaf – cut into 1cm (½") cubes
400g (14oz) endive or mixed salad leaves with endive
150g (5oz) creamy goats cheese
250ml (9fl oz) water
salt and pepper

This is a typical French salad with crisp endive and hot lardons (French cubed bacon), croutons and dressing. It can be passed around in a large salad bowl for people to help themselves or you can arrange it on individual serving plates.

Heat 2 tbsp of the oil in a large frying pan and fry the lardons or diced bacon for about 5 minutes or until golden and crispy. Remove with a slotted spoon and keep warm. Add the remaining 4 tbsp olive oil and fry the brioche cubes, turning frequently until golden. Remove and keep warm with the lardons. Add the goats cheese, water, salt and pepper to the frying pan, heat gently and stir until dissolved. Put endive or leaves in a large bowl with hot bacon and croutons and toss in dressing.

Cook's tip: If you don't want to fry the lardons and croutons at the last minute, you can do this earlier on in the day and serve them cold with hot dressing.

STUFFED TOULOUSE CHICKEN WITH A WALNUT SAUCE

2 handfuls fresh parsley – preferably flat leafed

100g (3½oz) walnut pieces

4 Toulouse sausages – remove skin

8 chicken breasts with skin

2 garlic cloves

1 tub (200ml) crème fraîche – the half fat type may be used

1 carton (284ml / ½pt) chicken stock

salt and pepper

Oven: 190°C, 375°F, Gas Mark 5

En route to our farmhouse, we spent a night in Toulouse. It's a very pretty town, full of interesting shops, restaurants and delicious sausages!

First put the parsley in a food processor to chop. Take ½ the parsley out of the food processor and mix with ¼ of the walnuts and the sausage meat. Make a slit in each chicken breast and open up like a book. Put sausage stuffing inside and fold chicken around.

To make the sauce put remaining walnuts and garlic in the food processor with the parsley and pulse to chop. Add crème fraîche, stock, salt and pepper and pulse again to mix.

◗ May be prepared up to this stage the day before.

Put chicken, skin side up, in an oven-proof dish or roasting tin and pour walnut sauce around. Cook in oven for 40 minutes, uncovered, basting occasionally.

Cook's tip: Other herby type sausages may be used instead of Toulouse sausages.

ROAST PROVENÇAL TOMATOES

2 slices brown bread

2 garlic cloves

3 handfuls basil

16 medium tomatoes

2 tbsp olive oil

salt and pepper

Oven: 190°C, 375°F, Gas Mark 5

These roast tomatoes are delicious eaten hot but can also be cooked in advance and served at room temperature.

Put bread, garlic and 2 handfuls of basil in a food processor to form breadcrumbs. Cut tomatoes in half through the equator and put in one layer, cut side up, in an oven proof serving dish. Sprinkle breadcrumb mixture on top. Drizzle with the olive oil and season.

❊ May be prepared earlier in the day.

Roast in oven for 30 minutes. Shred remaining handful of basil and sprinkle on top before serving.

NEW POTATOES IN GARLIC AND WINE

 In this recipe the potatoes are cooked in a stock with herbs and wine. During cooking they absorb all the wonderful flavours.

2 tbsp olive oil

1 large onion – chopped

2 garlic cloves – chopped

1.3kg (2lbs) small new potatoes

1 tbsp dried herbs de Provence

1 tbsp plain flour

300ml (½pt) chicken stock (made with 1 stock cube and boiling water)

1 glass white wine

salt and pepper

Heat oil in a very large saucepan, add chopped onions and garlic and sweat for 5 minutes to soften. Add potatoes, herbs and flour, mix together and cook for a few more minutes. Add stock and wine gradually, bring up to the boil, stirring every now and then, and simmer for 20 minutes. Season and serve.

✲ May be cooked earlier in the day.

To re-heat – put into any oven-proof gratin dish or serving dish, cover and put in oven: 190°C, 375°F, Gas Mark 5 for 30 minutes.

FEUILLETÉ WITH PRUNES IN ARMAGNAC AND CRÈME PÂTISSIÈRE

Most days, Carey Botting and I went down the road to the local "Boulangerie" to buy the bread. One day we got tempted by a scrumptious looking "gooey prune thing", so we bought it to analyse and this is what we came up with.

500g (1lb 2oz) ready soaked, pitted prunes – roughly chopped

6 tbsp Armagnac or brandy (or as much as you dare)

1 packet (375g) ready-rolled puff pastry

1 egg – beaten

2 tbsp brown sugar

1 carton (400ml) ready made custard (preferably fresh)

Oven: 200°C, 400°F, Gas Mark 6

Put chopped prunes in a bowl with the Armagnac and leave to marinate for at least 1 hour or longer.

Unroll the pastry and cut into 8 squares. With a sharp knife, mark the surface of the squares with a diamond pattern. Put onto a baking tray, brush with beaten egg and sprinkle with brown sugar. Put in oven for 20 minutes until golden and puffed up. Leave to cool.

◗ May be prepared up to this point the day before.

Cut pastry squares in half horizontally. Mix prunes with custard, spread on the pastry base and put the top back on.

ORDER OF PREPARATION IF MAKING IN ADVANCE:

The day before:
1. Prepare chicken up to ◗
2. Make pudding up to ◗

Earlier on the day:
3. Fry lardons and croutons.
4. Prepare tomatoes.
5. Cook potatoes.

In the evening:
6. Cook chicken as needed.
7. Cook tomatoes and re-heat potatoes.
8. Assemble feuilleté.
9. Make dressing for salad.

ORDER OF PREPARATION IN UNDER 90 MINUTES:

1. Make feuilleté up to ◗ and assemble before serving.
2. Put bread and garlic in food processor to make breadcrumbs for tomatoes (there's no need to wash processor before making chicken stuffing).
3. Prepare chicken and put in oven when necessary.
4. Prepare tomatoes and cook as needed.
5. Cook potatoes.
6. Make starter.

HEY PESTO

*P*esto *derives from the Italian word* pestare *meaning to pound or crush. Hey Presto comes from Latin* pestare *meaning ready. Put the two together and you have "ready in a crush" or better still, "ready in a rush"!*

8 globe artichokes
1 jar (250ml) hollandaise sauce
1 red pepper
1 garlic clove – crushed
salt and pepper

GLOBE ARTICHOKE WITH WARM RED PEPPER HOLLANDAISE

Globe artichokes are often thought of as being rather exotic and are unusually beautiful in appearance. They are rich in iron, minerals and vitamins and are low in calories. In fact, you may even feel you are burning up more calories in the effort it takes to eat them, pulling off each individual leaf and scraping off the soft fleshy base with your teeth, than the actual calorific intake! Dip the fleshy part of the leaf in the red pepper hollandaise as you go. Once you have pulled off all the leaves, you will find in the centre a hairy, spiky mass which is inedible and should be removed. Under this you will find the best part – the heart or base which is quite delectable and should be eaten with any remaining sauce – well worth waiting for. I prefer to serve the artichokes cold so that they can be prepared in advance. If you prefer, they can be cooked just before serving and eaten warm.

Trim the bases off the artichokes. Plunge into salted boiling water for 35 minutes (or until a base leave pulls away easily) and drain well.

To make the red pepper hollandaise – de-seed the red pepper, cut into chunks and put in a food processor to blend with the garlic, hollandaise sauce, salt and pepper.

◑ May be prepared the day before.

To warm red pepper hollandaise – put in microwave on low for 2 minutes. May be served in individual ramekin dishes with the artichokes at room temperature.

Cook's tip: Drain the artichokes upside down. Provide a large bowl in which your guests can dispose of their leaves.

SALMON AND PESTO FISH CAKES WITH A BULGUR WHEAT CRUST AND TOMATO, CAPER AND BASIL SALSA

140g (5oz) bulgur wheat

200ml (7fl oz) water

900g (2lbs) salmon fillet – skinned

8 spring onions

1 jar (190g) pesto

2 lemons

salt and pepper

TOMATO, CAPER AND BASIL SALSA

4 medium tomatoes – roughly chopped

1 tbsp olive oil

1 tbsp balsamic vinegar

½ tsp sugar

3 handfuls basil

1 jar capers – drained

salt and pepper

Oven: 220°C, 425°F, Gas Mark 7

Thanks to Gary Rhodes, fish cakes have now become the trendy dish to serve at dinner parties, rather than associate them with a snack to eat in front of the TV on a Sunday night! These are rather "classy" fish cakes made with salmon, taking on the Mediterranean flavours of pesto and nutty bulgur wheat. They are baked in the oven so you don't have to worry about smelling of fried fish for days afterwards.

Soak bulgur wheat in water for 10 minutes.

To make salsa – cut tomatoes into quarters and put in food processor with olive oil, balsamic vinegar, sugar and 2 handfuls of basil (reserve 1 for decoration). Pulse in food processor but do not blend too much as this is meant to be lumpy. Put in a bowl, add capers and season.

Trim spring onions and put in a food processor to roughly chop. Cut salmon into large chunks and add to food processor with pesto, juice of half a lemon, salt and pepper. Pulse food processor to mix ingredients but also leave lumpy.

Form into 16 cakes and roll in bulgur wheat. Keep refrigerated until needed.

◗ May be prepared up to this point the day before.

Put fish cakes on to a greased baking tray and cook in oven for 15 minutes.

Cut remaining 1½ lemons into wedges and use to garnish with remaining basil leaves. Serve with salsa.

Cook's tips: The easiest way to form the fish cakes is in your hands which tends to be a bit messy, but once they are rolled in the bulgur wheat they become firmer and easier to handle. If you haven't the time to make the salsa, buy a ready-made one instead.

MICROWAVE RISOTTO WITH WILD MUSHROOMS AND RED ONIONS

2 tbsp olive oil

1 red onion – chopped

200g (7oz) wild mushrooms – washed and sliced

400g (14oz) arborio or risotto rice

1.2 litres (2pts) vegetable or chicken stock (made with two stock cubes and boiling water)

salt and pepper

Why sweat over a hot frying pan cooking risotto, adding liquid drop by drop as most recipes tell you? I prefer to add all the drops at the same time, stick the risotto in the microwave and forget about it until I hear the "bleep bleep bleep". If you don't own a microwave, follow method described in Cashew Nut Risotto – see page 128.

Put olive oil and chopped onion in a large bowl suitable for microwaving. Cover with cling-film, leaving a gap for steam to escape, and microwave on high for 4 minutes. Add mushrooms and rice and mix well.

❋ May be prepared up to this point earlier in the day.

Add hot stock, cover and microwave on high for 20 minutes. Season and serve.

Cook's tip: The risotto can be cooked in the bowl in which it is going to be served as long as it is suitable for the microwave – anything to save washing up.

BROAD BEAN AND RADICCHIO SALAD

900g (2lbs) frozen broad beans

3 heads of radicchio (see Cook's tip below)

6 tbsp ready made French dressing

salt and pepper

A lovely colourful salad with a real crunch.

Cook broad beans according to instructions on the packet. Drain and toss in French dressing and season while hot.

◗ May be prepared up to this point the day before.

Put broad beans into a large salad bowl, tear or shred radicchio leaves and toss together.

Cook's tip: If you have problems finding radicchio heads, you can use a large bag of mixed leaves including radicchio instead.

NECTARINE AND RASPBERRY MASCARPONE GRATIN

6 ripe nectarines

250g (9oz) raspberries

2 egg yolks

2 tubs (250g each) mascarpone

1 pot (200g) Greek yoghurt

large slug Marsala or port

(approx 4 tbsp)

4 tbsp brown sugar

Oven: 190°C, 375°F, Gas Mark 5

I love the combination of these two summer fruits and together with mascarpone and brown sugar they are quite irresistible.

Cut nectarines in quarters, remove the stone and slice. Put into one large gratin dish or 8 individual ones with the raspberries. Beat egg yolks together with mascarpone, Greek yoghurt and Marsala or port. Pour over the fruit and sprinkle brown sugar on top.

☀ May be prepared up to this point earlier in the day.

Cook in oven for 30 minutes in a large dish, or 20 minutes in individual dishes, and serve.

Cook's tip: If nectarines and raspberries are not in season, you can use frozen raspberries and substitute the nectarines with 2 large mangoes.

ORDER OF PREPARATION IF MAKING IN ADVANCE:

The day before:
1. Cook artichokes and make red pepper hollandaise (don't bother to wash the food processor before using it for the salsa, then fish cakes).
2. Make salsa and fish cakes.
3. Prepare broad bean salad up to ◖

Earlier on the day:
4. Prepare microwave risotto to ☀
5. Prepare mascarpone gratin up to ☀

In the evening:
6. Heat hollandaise as necessary.
7. Add stock to risotto and put in microwave.
8. Cook fish cakes.
9. Finish off salad.
10. Put gratin in oven while eating main course.

ORDER OF PREPARATION IN UNDER 90 MINUTES:

1. Cook artichokes and make red pepper hollandaise (don't wash food processor).
2. Make salsa then fish cakes and cook as needed.
3. Prepare broad bean salad and toss in radicchio before serving.
4. Prepare mascarpone gratin and cook while eating main course.
5. Make risotto.

VEGETARIANS OF THE ORIENT

*♀ A New World Riesling.
Recommendation – Jim Barry Lodge
Hill Riesling from Australia*

*A*s oriental cooking has become so popular and with more and more people becoming vegetarians, I thought I'd combine the two and have come up with "Vegetarians of the Orient" (not that I'm actually cooking the vegetarians!). As with all my recipes, I tried this out on Nick, my husband (he's still as thin as ever and never seems to put on weight). Nick is a real meat eater and not over keen on very spicy food, so I was very surprised when he said it was one of the nicest curries he's ever eaten. He still talks about the wonderful "chicken" and coconut curry and asks when I'm going to make it again – I don't like to disillusion him!

ORIENTAL ROAST VEGETABLE
SATAY ON POPPADOMS

1 cauliflower – cut stalks off and separate into florets

3 yellow courgettes – thickly sliced (green courgettes may be used instead)

1 aubergine – cut into large chunks

2 medium leeks – thickly sliced

2 red peppers – de-seeded and thickly sliced

4 tbsp sesame oil

salt and pepper

1 jar (200g) satay sauce (Sharwoods recommended)

8 ready-made poppadoms

Oven: 220°C, 425°F, Gas Mark 7

 Roasting vegetables in sesame oil gives them wonderful flavours and the satay sauce has a spicy bite to it.

Prepare vegetables and put into a large roasting dish. Toss in sesame oil and season.

※ May be prepared up to this point earlier in the day.

Cook in oven for 45 minutes, tossing half way though. Heat satay sauce according to instructions on the jar.

Put one poppadom on each plate, pile roast vegetables in the middle and pour satay sauce on top.

Cook's tip: There is no need to heat the poppadoms as the heat from the vegetables is enough to warm them.

THAI QUORN CURRY WITH COCONUT AND MANGO

2 onions
2 cloves garlic
3cm (1¼") cube fresh ginger
1 - 2 green chillies – de-seeded
3 handfuls coriander
2 tbsp ground nut oil
2 tins (400g each) coconut milk
700g (1lb 9oz) quorn pieces
1 large mango – peeled and cut into chunks
3 limes
salt and pepper

Quorn comes from a natural, tiny plant. It is actually a fungus and a distant relative of the mushroom. It is found in the soil in and around Marlow in Buckinghamshire. It is low in fat and high in protein and fibre. Even though Quorn is pretty tasteless on it's own, marinated or mixed with strong flavoured ingredients, it takes on their tastes and becomes quite delicious.

Finely chop the onions, garlic, ginger, chilli and 2 handfuls of the coriander (may be done in a food processor).

Heat the oil in a large saucepan. Add the chopped ingredients as above and sauté for a couple of minutes. Add the coconut milk, quorn and zest and juice of one lime.

◑ May be prepared up to this point the day before.

Bring quorn curry up to boil and then allow to simmer gently for 20 minutes. Add the mango, salt and pepper and continue to cook for a further 10 minutes.

Chop remaining coriander and cut remaining limes into wedges. Serve quorn curry with coriander sprinkled on top and a wedge of lime.

Cook's tip: For non-vegetarians, this could be made with prawns instead of Quorn. Use 900g (2lbs) uncooked prawns and cook in the same way as above but do not add the prawns until just before cooking.

BASMATI RICE WITH MINT AND CUMIN

400g (14oz) basmati rice
1 vegetable stock cube
3 tsp cumin seeds
2 handfuls chopped mint
salt and pepper

Basmati means "the fragrant one", the mint and cumin make it just a little more so.

Cook rice according to instructions on packet but add the stock cube and cumin seeds. When cooked, add chopped mint and season.

Cook's tip: If cooking in the microwave, use a microwavable serving bowl so that you can take it straight from the microwave to the table and also save yourself some washing up.

STIR-FRY BROCCOLI AND BABY CORN WITH SESAME SEEDS

2 tbsp sesame oil

1kg (2lbs 4oz) broccoli

8 spring onions

250g (9oz) baby corn

4 tbsp soy sauce

4 tbsp sesame seeds

These vegetables are quickly stir-fried to preserve crispness and colour.

Thinly slice the stalks of the broccoli on the diagonal and break the heads up into florets. Slice the spring onions on the diagonal.

Heat sesame oil in a wok. Add broccoli, spring onions and baby corn. Stir fry for 5 minutes, add soy sauce and sesame seeds, continue to stir-fry for a further 3 minutes and serve.

Cook's tip: This may be served straight from the wok.

ICED BANOFFI AND BANANA TERRINE WITH A RUM AND BUTTERSCOTCH SAUCE

2 packets butterscotch flavoured Angel Delight (the sugar-free one may be used)

1 tin (400g) condensed milk

20 ginger snap biscuits (200g) – roughly crushed

1 bottle butterscotch sauce ("Smuckers" recommended)

large slug rum (approx 4 tbsp)

3 bananas

Who didn't enjoy Angel Delight as a child? Whether or not you did, you'll love this and no one will ever guess what it's made out of. Keep it your secret and don't tell a soul (or even an angel).

Line a 1.5 litre terrine tin or loaf tin with cling film. Make the Angel Delight as instructions on packet. Whisk in the condensed milk and fold in the crushed biscuits. Put into prepared terrine tin and freeze for at least 3 hours. Mix butterscotch sauce with rum.

❅ The terrine may be kept in a freezer for up to 3 months.

◗ The butterscotch sauce may be made the day before.

To serve – turn banoffi terrine out of tin and place on a long serving plate. Slice bananas and pile on top and around the terrine. Slice and serve with butterscotch sauce.

ORDER OF PREPARATION IF MAKING IN ADVANCE:

The day before:
1. Prepare Quorn curry up to ◗
2. Make iced banoffi terrine and rum and butterscotch sauce.
   Earlier on the day:
3. Prepare roast vegetables up to ❅

In the evening:
4. Put roast vegetables in oven and heat satay sauce as needed.
5. Prepare vegetables for stir-fry and cook as necessary.
6. Finish off cooking Quorn curry.
7. Cook rice.
8. Slice bananas and serve with banoffi terrine.

ORDER OF PREPARATION IN UNDER 90 MINUTES:

1. Make banoffi terrine and sauce.
2. Prepare roast vegetables and cook as necessary.
3. Make curry.
4. Prepare vegetables for stir-fry and cook as necessary.
5. Cook rice.

Opposite: Cancun Cooking (page 130)

A DINNER PARTY FOR THE AGA

A friend recently rang me in a panic to ask for help as she, her family and friends (12 in total) were going on holiday to Wales and renting a cottage which only had an Aga. As I have been the proud owner of an Aga for just over a year, I was able to give her some useful tips. As a result, I thought it was a good idea to include an Aga menu in my book for those of you who own one or those who occasionally cook on them.

GRILLED AUBERGINE AND HALLOUMI CAKE WITH A SPICY CUCUMBER DRESSING

3 tbsp olive oil for brushing

2 large aubergines – each sliced into 8 rounds

500g (1lb 2oz) Halloumi cheese – cut into 16 slices

4 medium tomatoes – each sliced into 4 with ends discarded

300g (10oz) ready-made tzatziki

1 green chilli – de-seeded and finely chopped

100g bag of mixed salad leaves

Halloumi is a Greek cheese, similar to feta but has more of an elastic texture. It is delicious cooked but should be eaten while hot as once cooled, it becomes rubbery. In this recipe, it is layered with aubergine and tomato slices to form a "cake" and makes an attractive and colourful starter.

Brush both sides of the aubergine slices with oil and season. Place in one layer on a rack, over a large roasting tin and hang the tin on the top set of runners in the roasting oven. Cook for 20 minutes, turning half way through. Meanwhile, mix the chopped chilli with the tzatziki. To make each cake, put a round of aubergine on the bottom, followed by a slice of halloumi, tomato, aubergine, halloumi and finish off with tomato. Repeat the same process 7 more times until you have 8 cakes.

❄ May be prepared up to this stage earlier in the day.

Brush a baking tray or roasting tin with oil to grease. Put the cakes on the tray and put in roasting oven on third set of runners for 10 minutes. Serve hot with the salad leaves and spicy cucumber dressing.

Cook's tip: A few drops of chilli sauce may be used instead of the fresh chilli.

Opposite: Finger Food In A Flash
(page 136)

MUSTARD AND GINGER MARINATED LAMB MEDALLIONS ****

4 tsp wholegrain mustard

4 tbsp ginger conserve

2 cans (275ml) "Mackeson" beer

5 lamb neck fillets

2 tbsp plain flour

2 tbsp olive oil

salt and pepper

In this recipe I have used lamb neck fillets which become beautifully tender, juicy and succulent when cooked slowly.

Mix together mustard, ginger conserve and Mackeson and pour over lamb. Leave to marinate in a non-metallic dish for at least 30 minutes or preferably over night.

◑ May be prepared up to this stage the day before.

Mix the flour with salt and pepper, remove the lamb from the marinade and coat with seasoned flour. Put the oil in a heavy flame-proof casserole dish or frying pan and heat on the boiling plate. Add the lamb and brown on all sides, moving to the simmering plate if it is spitting too much. Add the marinade, bring up to the boil and allow to simmer gently for 10 minutes. Cover and place in the simmering oven for 1½ hours.

To serve – slice the lamb and serve with the sauce.

Cook's tip: When cooking for large numbers and often opening the lids on the top plates, the Aga tends to lose some heat. I compensate for this by turning up the thermostat a couple of hours before I start cooking, but remember to turn it down afterwards.

ORANGE, PINE NUT AND RAISIN PILAFF

2 tbsp olive oil

1 large onion – chopped

400g (14oz) long grain rice

1 carton frozen concentrated orange juice with water added to make up to 750ml (1¼ pts)

100g (3½oz) pine nuts

4 tbsp raisins

salt and pepper

In this recipe, the rice is cooked in orange juice, giving it a lovely flavour and the addition of the pine nuts and raisins makes a colourful dish. The Aga is great for cooking rice as it can be cooked in the simmering oven and if it is left a little longer than planned, it will still stay moist.

Heat the oil in a saucepan (preferably "Agalux" – see Cook's tip below) or a flame-proof casserole on the boiling plate. Add the onion, transfer to the simmering plate and fry gently for about 5 minutes, adding the pine nuts for the last 2 minutes. Add rice, raisins, salt and pepper and stir to coat in the oil.

☼ May be prepared up to this stage earlier in the day.

Add the orange juice and water, bring up to boiling on the boiling plate. Cover the pan or casserole and put on the floor of the simmering oven for 20 minutes.

Cook's tip: Agalux pans (oven-proof pans) are ideal for this recipe as you can start cooking on top of the Aga and transfer the pan to the bottom oven.

ROASTED ROOT VEGETABLES WITH CORIANDER

1 small swede – peeled and cut into chunks

5 large carrots – scrubbed and thickly sliced

2 medium sized potatoes – scrubbed and cut into chunks

2 onions – peeled and cut into eighths

2 garlic cloves – sliced

2 handfuls coriander – chopped

4 tbsp olive oil

salt and pepper

Roasted vegetables have become very popular. Not only do they taste wonderful (especially cooked in the Aga) but they are easy to prepare.

Put all ingredients in a large roasting tin and hang on the top set of runners in the roasting oven. Cook for 1 hour, tossing half way through.

Cook's tip: I find when roasting in the Aga, food tends to stick in the roasting tin and make it difficult to wash up afterwards. I would recommend using "Bake-O-Glide", a re-usable Teflon coated baking parchment, to line the tin.

PEAR AND ALMOND TART

375g ready-made short crust pastry – preferably dessert pastry

1 large tin (800g) pears – well drained

200g (7oz) ground almonds

110g (4oz) caster sugar

3 eggs

115g (4oz) butter

1 tub (200ml) crème fraîche or Greek yoghurt

Oven: 190°C, 375°F, Gas Mark 5

One of the many great advantages of cooking in an Aga is that you can cook tarts and quiches without first having to bake the pastry blind as it cooks from the heat on the base of the oven. I prefer to serve this tart warm but it can also be served cold.

You will need a flan tin (preferably loose bottomed) approx 28cm (11").

Roll out the pastry, line the flan tin and prick the base with a fork. Arrange the pears on the pastry, rounded side up. Put the ground almonds, sugar, eggs and butter in a food processor to blend and pour over the pears. Cook on the base of the roasting oven for 20 minutes. Serve hot with crème fraîche or Greek yoghurt.

❄ May be made the day before or may be frozen.

To re-heat – put in simmering oven for 20 minutes.

ORDER OF PREPARATION IF MAKING IN ADVANCE:

The day before:
1. Marinate lamb.
2. Make pear and almond tart.

Earlier in the day:
3. Prepare aubergine and halloumi cake up to ❄
4. Prepare rice up to ❄

In the evening:
5. Cook lamb.
6. Prepare root vegetables and put in oven as needed.
7. Cook rice.
8. Put aubergine cake in oven.
9. Re-heat tart.

ORDER OF PREPARATION IN UNDER 90 MINUTES:

1. Marinate lamb for 30 minutes and then cook.
2. Cook vegetables.
3. Prepare aubergine cakes and put in oven as needed.
4. Cook rice.
5. Make tart but don't cook until 20 minutes before you need it.

HALLOWEEN

*T**his is a lovely warming menu to eat on a cold chilly night, which surprisingly is relatively low in calories. It's ideal for Halloween.*

LEEK AND BROCCOLI SOUP WITH ROQUEFORT CROUTONS

The combination of the cheese with the leeks and broccoli is quite delicious.

800g (1lb 12oz) leeks
600g (1lb 5oz) broccoli
1.2 litres (2pts) vegetable or chicken stock (made with 2 stock cubes and boiling water)
300ml (½pt) milk
salt and pepper
1 baguette
175g (6oz) Roquefort or other cheeses such as Stilton, Gorgonzola or chèvre

Slice leeks, break broccoli into florets and slice stalks. Put in a large saucepan with stock, bring up to boil and simmer for 20 minutes. Blend in a liquidizer or food processor, add milk and season.

◐ May be made the day before.

✳ May be frozen.

To make croutons – cut baguette into 24 thin slices (approx. 1cm/ ½" thick). Crumble roquefort on top.

☀ The croutons may be prepared earlier in the day.

Either put croutons on a baking tray and put in oven: 190°C, 375°F, Gas Mark 5 for 10 minutes or put under a pre-heated grill until cheese bubbles.
Re-heat soup gently in the saucepan until piping hot. Serve soup with hot croutons.

DEVILLED PORK MEDALLIONS

"Devilled" means to cook with hot or spicy seasonings. Of course you could always serve devils on horseback and devils food cake on Halloween too.

3 pork tenderloin (approx. 1.2kg (2lbs 12oz) in total)
1 small pot (150g) plain yoghurt
paprika
MARINADE
3 tbsp marmalade
2 tbsp Worcester sauce
2 tbsp tomato ketchup
1 tbsp curry powder
1 tsp French mustard
3cm (1¼") cube fresh ginger – peeled and chopped
3 garlic cloves – chopped
2 lemons – zest and juice
1 tbsp olive oil
salt and pepper
Oven: 200°C, 400°F, Gas Mark 6

Mix all marinade ingredients together and pour over pork fillets. Leave to marinate for at least 45 minutes or as long as possible.

◐ May be made up to this stage the day before.

Put pork with marinade in a roasting dish and cook in oven, uncovered, for 40-45 minutes, basting with marinade half way though cooking.

To serve – slice the pork into medallions and arrange in a circle on each plate. Put a blob of yoghurt on top and sprinkle with paprika.

CHILLI AND CORIANDER MASH

1.5kg (3lbs 5oz) potatoes

1 red chilli – de-seeded and finely chopped (or a few drops chilli sauce)

2 handfuls fresh chopped coriander

3 tbsp olive oil

300ml (½pt) milk

salt and pepper

My husband's favourite way of eating potatoes is mashed. I have even known him to bribe the chef in our favourite local Italian restaurant with a bottle of Champagne if he would make him mashed potato (it turned out to be an expensive evening)! He's delighted that this wonderful "comfort food" has now become so "trendy" that it can be served at dinner parties.

Peel potatoes and boil until soft. Drain and mash together with remaining ingredients but reserving one handful of coriander.

☼ May be made earlier in the day.

To re-heat – microwave on high for 8 minutes, stirring half way through. Sprinkle remaining chopped coriander on top and serve.

Cook's tip: If re-heating, more milk may need to be added to maintain a creamy consistency.

ROAST PUMPKIN WITH CINNAMON AND BROWN SUGAR

1 pumpkin – approx 1.6kg (3lbs 8oz)

2 tbsp brown sugar

2 tsp cinnamon

25g (1oz) butter

salt and pepper

Oven: 200°C, 400°F, Gas Mark 6

I am delighted that pumpkins are now eaten in this country rather than only used as Halloween decorations. I am also pleased to see that so many other squashes are now available in the shops. I have decided to roast the pumpkin in this recipe with brown sugar and cinnamon to bring out its natural tender nutty flavour.

Peel pumpkin, cut in half, scoop out the seeds and cut flesh into large chunks.

Put into a roasting dish, sprinkle sugar and cinnamon on, dot with butter and season. Put in oven, uncovered, for 35-45 minutes or until tender. Toss half way through cooking.

Cook's tip: If you are cooking this menu for Halloween, why not buy 2 pumpkins and use one to hollow out and put a candle inside?

TARTE A L'ORANGE

250g (9oz) ready-made short crust pastry

2 large oranges

115g (4oz) caster sugar

500g (1lb 2oz) Greek yoghurt

3 eggs

1 tbsp icing sugar

Oven: 180°C, 350°F, Gas Mark 4

Due to the popularity of my "Tarte au Citron" in my first book, I have been asked by many people to create a similar type. I have come up with this orange tarte, to provide a cleansing and refreshing dessert.

Roll out pastry and line a tart tin or flan dish, 28cm (11") in diameter, preferably loose-bottomed. Prick the base with a fork and put in freezer for 10 minutes to chill. Take out of freezer and put in oven for 12 minutes.

Meanwhile, put one whole orange (zest, pith and everything) in a food processor to blend until smooth. Add the zest and juice of the other orange, sugar, half the Greek yoghurt and eggs to blend. Pour into pastry case and put back in oven for 30 minutes. Either serve immediately (see serving suggestions below) or leave to cool and store in fridge overnight.

◗ May be made the day before.

To re-heat – put in oven for 15 minutes.

To serve – remove sides of tin if necessary and put on a serving plate. Dust with icing sugar, slice and serve with remaining yoghurt.

Cook's tip: For a real Halloween feel, this tarte could be served with sliced blood oranges.

ORDER OF PREPARATION IF MAKING IN ADVANCE:

The day before:
1. Marinate pork.
2. Make soup.
3. Make tarte.

Earlier on the day:
4. Prepare croutons up to ☀
5. Make mash.

In the evening:
6. Prepare pumpkin and put in oven as needed.
7. Cook pork as needed.
8. Re-heat soup and cook croutons.
9. Re-heat potato.
10. Re-heat tarte.

ORDER OF PREPARATION IN UNDER 90 MINUTES:

1. Marinate pork and cook as necessary.
2. Prepare pumpkin and cook as needed.
3. Prepare pastry case and filling for tarte but there's no need to put it in the oven until you are eating your main course (30 minutes before you're going to serve it).
4. Make soup and prepare croutons.
5. Make mash.

BUBBLY BRUNCH

♀ New World Fizz.
Recommendation – Lindauer Special
Reserve from New Zealand
Full bodied, New World Chardonnay.
Recommendation – Deakin Estate
Chardonnay from Australia

*B*runches are becoming more and more popular because they provide a casual way to entertain friends. Formal "stuffy" Sunday lunches, where you feel you should provide 25 different vegetables, the roast beef gets burnt and Yorkshire puddings sink because your guests are late, can be a nightmare. Why not invite them for brunch instead and enjoy a few bottles of bubbly along the way.

STEAMING HOT BLOODY MARY SOUP WITH WARM CHEESE STRAWS

2 litres (3½pts) tomato juice

1 tin (400g) chopped tomatoes

3 tbsp Worcester sauce

few drops Tabasco (to taste)

juice 1 lemon

2 tsp sugar

celery salt and pepper

1 handful fresh chopped parsley

4 sticks celery – cut in half length ways

vodka

2 packets cheese straws

This is a lovely spicy soup to cure any hang-over. I like to serve it in mugs or cups and pass the vodka to each person to help themselves to the amount they want. The celery is used as a stirrer.

The cheese straws are a real cheat but putting them in the oven to warm convinces people that they are home-made!

Mix all soup ingredients together except the parsley, celery and vodka.

◑ May be prepared up to this stage the day before.

Heat the soup in a saucepan over a gentle heat for approximately 15 minutes, stirring occasionally, until piping hot.
Meanwhile put cheese straws on a baking tray and put in oven: 190°C, 375°F, Gas Mark 5 for 5 minutes to warm. Pour soup into mugs, cups or soup bowls, sprinkle chopped parsley on top and put half a stick of celery in each one. Allow your guests to add the vodka themselves and serve with warm cheese straws.

Cook's tip: The spiciness of the soup is determined by the amount of Worcester sauce and Tabasco so taste the soup as you go along.

SMOKED HADDOCK WITH A BÉARNAISE SAUCE

900g (2lbs) smoked haddock or smoked cod fillets – skinned

1 jar (250ml) béarnaise sauce

Oven: 190°C, 375°F, Gas Mark 5

This recipe can also be made using smoked cod and you can either use dyed or undyed fish. The smokiness of the fish is quite delicious with the béarnaise sauce.

Cut smoked haddock into 8 portions, remove bones if necessary. Put in a roasting dish (preferably in one layer) and cover with water. Put in oven for 15 minutes. Heat béarnaise sauce by putting it in a microwave on defrost for 2 minutes or heat according to instructions on jar. Drain smoked haddock and serve with béarnaise sauce poured on top.

CASHEW NUT RISOTTO

2 tbsp olive oil

1 large onion – chopped

400g (14oz) risotto rice

1.5 litres (2¾pts) hot vegetable or fish stock – can be made using 2 stock cubes and boiling water

100g (3½oz) roasted, salted cashew nuts

55g (2oz) butter

salt and pepper

I absolutely adore risotto and have even been known to eat it four days in a row. My only dislike is the conventional method of making risotto by adding the liquid drop by drop and stirring continuously for 30 minutes (too time consuming for "Dinners in a Dash"). My method is somewhat unconventional as I add the liquid in one go and stir as often as I remember – it tastes just as good but without all the hassles. For other unconventional methods of cooking risotto, see pages 116 and 18, for microwave and oven cooked versions.

Heat the oil in a large saucepan. Add the chopped onion and fry gently for 5 minutes. Add rice, cook for a further minute then add the hot stock. Bring up to the boil and allow to simmer, stirring every now and then, for about 20 minutes or until rice is tender. Add cashew nuts, butter and season to taste.

◗ May be prepared the day before.

To re-heat - put in microwave on high for 7 minutes.

Cook's tip: If you make the risotto in advance, you may need to add some extra stock when re-heating to prevent it drying out and keep it moist and creamy.

RED CABBAGE, APPLE AND CARAWAY SALAD

1 medium red cabbage

3 red apples

4 handfuls raisins or currants

3 tsp caraway seeds

8 tbsp ready-made French Dressing

salt and pepper

This really crunchy salad with vibrant red colours is ideal to serve in the winter.

Shred the cabbage, core the apples and cut into chunks. Mix together in a large salad bowl with all other ingredients.

◗ May be prepared earlier in the day.

SPICED CIDER FRUIT COMPOTE WITH YOGHURT AND BLUEBERRY MUFFINS

500g (1lb 2oz) mixed dried fruits (see Cook's tip below)

600ml (1pt) cider

1 mulled wine sachet or 2 tsp cinnamon

500g (1lb 2oz) Greek Yoghurt

1 packet blueberry muffin mix – "Berry Crocker" recommended or 8 ready-made muffins

Just as you are recovering from your hang-over, this will help restore your alcohol level. If you are worried that the level of "blood in your wine stream" may be getting too low, see cook's tip below! The blueberry muffins are a real cheat but "Betty" does make some excellent ones or if you want to cheat even more, buy them ready-made and just heat them up to give them that real home-made feeling.

Put cider, mulled wine sachet or cinnamon and dried fruit in a saucepan and simmer for 15 minutes. Remove mulled wine sachet and leave to cool. Cook muffins according to instructions on packet.

◗ May be made the day before.

Put muffins in oven: 190°C, 375°F, Gas Mark 5 for 10 minutes to warm and serve with fruit compote and Greek yoghurt.

Cook's tips: You can either mix your own fruits, e.g. dried apricots, figs, dates, peaches, or buy a packet of ready mixed dried fruits. The cider may be replaced by apple juice.

ORDER OF PREPARATION IF MAKING IN ADVANCE:

The day before:
1. Make soup.
2. Make risotto.
3. Make pudding up to ◗

Earlier on the day:
3. Make salad.

Later in the morning:
4. Heat soup and cheese straws.
5. Cook fish and heat béarnaise sauce.
6. Re-heat risotto.
7. Re-heat muffins.

ORDER OF PREPARATION IN UNDER 90 MINUTES:

1. Make fruit compote and muffins. Re-heat muffins if necessary.
2. Make salad.
3. Prepare soup and cheese straws and heat as required.
4. Make risotto.
5. Cook fish and heat béarnaise sauce.

CANCUN COOKING

A ripe, New World white and red. Recommendations – Isla Negra Chardonnay from Chile. Redwood Trail Cabernet Sauvignon from California

Cancun is a beautiful island in the Yucatan, off the East coast of Mexico. The following menu has been slightly Westernised to suit our more delicate palate (in other words the amount of chilli won't blow your head off) and is definitely more sophisticated than the type of rustic island food that you might eat there. The menu is very impressive but I can assure you, very easy and if I can cook it virtually with my eyes closed, then you "cancun" cook it easily as well.

TORTILLA BASKETS WITH PRAWN, AVOCADO AND TOMATO SALSA

I have often been to Mexican restaurants in England and seen salads served in deep fried tortilla baskets. They look pretty but tend to be rather greasy. As I don't own a deep fat fryer, I set about trying to create a tortilla basket with the same look but without the frying or greasiness and came up with this simple yet very effective and impressive idea.

8 small wheat tortillas

1 avocado – peeled and roughly chopped

juice of ½ lime plus 2 limes for decoration

1 green pepper – de-seeded and roughly chopped

8 spring onions – sliced

300g (10½oz) frozen prawns – de-frosted

1 jar (approx 250g) ready-made tomato salsa

2 little gem lettuces

salt and pepper

Oven: 180°C, 350°F, Gas Mark 4

To make the tortilla baskets you will need to use bowls as moulds, anything from 12cm-14cm (4 ½-5 ½") in diameter. Push the tortilla down into the bowls (if you don't have 8 bowls then make them in batches). Put tortilla filled bowls in the oven for 15 minutes. Remove from bowl and allow to cool.

◗ May be made up to 2 days in advance and kept in an air-tight container.

To make filling – put chopped avocado in a bowl with the juice of ½ lime, green pepper, spring onions, prawns and salsa and mix together.

☼ May be prepared earlier in the day.

To serve – shred the lettuce and put in the bottom of the baskets. Put the avocado mixture on top. Cut limes into wedges and serve on the side.

Cook's tip: If you want to take a real short cut, buy the ready-made tortillas shells and stuff filling inside. They won't look as impressive but will save time if you're in a real hurry.

VENISON CHILLI WITH CRÈME FRAÎCHE AND CORIANDER

1 tbsp olive oil

1 large onion – chopped

2 garlic cloves – chopped or crushed

1kg (2lbs 4oz) venison mince
(or diced venison which you can mince
in a food processor)

2 tsp cumin seeds

1 jar (approx 350g) chilli cooking
sauce (see Cook's tip)

1 tin (400g) chopped tomatoes

300ml (14fl oz) Mexican or light
American beer

4 tbsp tomato purée

2 red peppers – de-seeded and sliced

2 tins (400g each) red kidney beans

1 tsp sugar

1 tub (200ml) crème fraîche –
the half fat type may be used

2 handfuls fresh chopped coriander

salt and pepper

Last year we went skiing to Deer Valley, Utah with our great friends David and Chris Gustafson. I picked up some wonderful ideas for unusual recipes and venison chilli was one of them. Utah, being a Mormon State, is lacking in alcohol so I'm sure my recipe is somewhat different, easier and I'm certain the one there didn't include any beer!

Heat the oil in a very large frying pan. Add the chopped onion and fry for about 5 minutes until soft. Add garlic, venison and cumin seeds and cook for a further 5 minutes to brown. Add all other ingredients except the crème fraîche and coriander and allow to simmer gently for 45 minutes, stirring occasionally.

◗ May be made the day before.

❊ May be frozen.

If making in advance, re-heat until piping hot. Serve with a blob of crème fraîche and coriander sprinkled on top.

Cook's tip: There are quite a few chilli cooking sauces around. I recommend Loyd Grossman's Tomato and Chilli Sauce or Sainsburys own brand. This recipe is ideal for large numbers and great for parties as you can make it in advance. It can be served in the tortilla baskets (above) instead of the avocado and prawns. It can also be made into a vegetarian chilli by substituting 2 cubed aubergines and 3 sliced courgettes for the venison.

ROAST SWEET CORN AND RED ONIONS

4 red onions – peeled and
cut in quarters

4 corn on the cob – cut in half

2 tbsp olive oil

salt and pepper

Oven: 200°C, 400°F, Gas Mark 6

½

I love barbecued sweet corn as it brings out the juicy nuttiness in them. Roasting has a similar effect and is delicious with the roast red onion.

Put all ingredients in a large roasting tin and mix together. Roast in oven for 45 minutes, tossing half way through.

Cook's tip: If corn on the cob is not in season, then frozen corn on the cob may be used instead and cooked straight from the freezer.

CHEESY BAKED POTATO WEDGES

1.5kg (3lbs 5oz) large potatoes

2tbsp olive oil

2 tbsp grated Parmesan

salt and pepper

Oven: 200°C, 400°F, Gas Mark 6

 These are similar to deep fried potato skins but have got more bite to them and are a bit healthier cooked this way.

Scrub potatoes and cut each into 6 wedges. Put in a large roasting tin and mix with olive oil, Parmesan and seasoning. Cook for 1 – 1 ¼ hours, until crisp, tossing occasionally.

BANANA, MANGO,
FUDGE AND RUM BRULÉE

1 small pot (150g) ready-made custard

100g (3½oz) fudge – or about
10 pieces

1 small mango – peeled and
cut into chunks

2 bananas – peeled and sliced

juice of ½ lemon

300ml (½pt) double cream

4 tbsp dark rum

8 tbsp brown sugar

One of the perks of being a cookery writer is having to taste all the recipes – usually just a small taste, but in this case the tasting lasted a long time!

Put custard and fudge into a saucepan and heat gently, stirring occasionally until fudge has melted. Leave to cool slightly.

Put mango and bananas in a large bowl and mix with lemon juice. Whisk the cream with the rum until thick. Fold all ingredients in together and either put into 8 ramekin dishes or one large gratin dish. Sprinkle over the brown sugar. Put under a pre-heated grill on maximum for 3-4 minutes or until bubbling. Chill for at least one hour.

◗ May be made the day before.

Cook's tip: This is a handy recipe to make if you're doing some decorating. If you're using a blow torch to strip paint, just stop for a minute and put it on your crème brulée to melt and brown the topping then you can go back to stripping!

ORDER OF PREPARATION IF MAKING
IN ADVANCE:

The day before:
1. Make tortilla baskets.
2. Make venison chilli.
3. Make brulée.

Earlier on the day:
4. Mix filling for tortilla baskets.

In the evening:
5. Prepare and cook potatoes.
6. Prepare and roast corn and onion.
7. Re-heat chilli.
8. Assemble starter.

ORDER OF PREPARATION IN
UNDER 90 MINUTES:

1. Prepare and cook potatoes.
2. Prepare and roast vegetables as needed.
3. Make chilli.
4. Make brulée.
5. Make starter.

PERFECT POT ROAST

*P*ot roasts are so easy to prepare, cook and need only the minimum of attention. As all the ingredients are cooked together in one dish, there's little washing up to do at the end. In my recipe I have used guinea fowl which was given its name because it originated as a game bird, native to the Guinea coast of West Africa. The guinea fowl has now been domesticated in Europe for over 500 years. It's a cross between a chicken and a pheasant, being more tender than a pheasant and darker and "gamier" than a chicken.

6 leeks - sliced

1 tub (200ml) crème fraiche – the low
fat type may be used

175g (6oz) Stilton –
crumbled or grated

2 packets (25g each) cheese and onion
crisps - crushed

salt and pepper

LEEK AND STILTON CRUMBLE

I remember, about 20 years ago (I was only a small kid but a good cook with a long memory!) making a chicken recipe, using crisps. Not only was it considered very trendy but also was quite yummy. I have decided to reincarnate the crisp topping – it creates a lovely combination of textures with the leeks, saves the time it would take to make a proper crumble topping and, if you buy an extra packet of crisps, you can eat them while you make this recipe.

Put sliced leeks into boiling water and simmer for 5 minutes. Drain well and mix with crème fraiche, Stilton and seasoning. Put in ramekin or small gratin dishes and sprinkle crushed crisps on top. Put under a grill for 3 - 4 minutes to brown.

◑ May be made the day before.

If making in advance, do not put the crisps on top or grill. Add the crisps in the evening and put the ramekin or gratin dishes in oven: 190°C, 375°F, Gas Mark 5 for 20 minutes.

Cook's tip: To crush crisps, leave in bag and pound them with your fist. This recipe is also good to make as a main course for a casual lunch. Just double the quantities and serve with a crisp green salad and warm crusty bread.

POT ROAST GUINEA FOWL WITH PANCETTA ON A BED OF BARLEY RISOTTO WITH WILD MUSHROOMS

2 guinea fowl – each weighing approx. 1.5kg (3lbs 5oz) – jointed into 4 pieces each (see Cook's tips)

400g (14oz) pearl barley

40g (1½oz) dried wild mushrooms

2.2 litres (3¾pts) chicken stock – made with 3 chicken stock cubes and boiling water

16 slices (160g / 6oz) pancetta

4 red onions – cut in quarters

16 kumquats – cut in half

pepper

Oven: 200°C, 400°F, Gas Mark 6

 I remember as a child, my Mother making wonderful warming barley soups – she tells me she still makes them now. Barley is something that seems to have been forgotten but is always popular and makes a lovely change from rice, pasta or potatoes.

You will need a very large, wide casserole or roasting tin (or alternatively use two).

Put the barley into the casserole, add the dried mushrooms, pour over the hot stock and season with pepper. Lay the guinea fowl portions on top in one layer with 2 slices of pancetta on top of each portion. Tuck the onion quarters in between the guinea fowl. Cover and put in oven for 1 hour. After the first 30 minutes add the kumquats and leave uncovered for the pancetta to crisp up for the last 30 minutes.

Cook's tips: Guinea fowl are tougher to joint than chickens. You will need a very sharp knife or poultry sheers or ask your butcher to do it for you. Bacon may be used instead of pancetta if preferred.

RED CABBAGE IN MULLED WINE

1 large onion – sliced

1 large red cabbage – coarsely shredded

2 glasses red wine

2 tbsp brown sugar

1 tsp cinnamon

1 tsp ground ginger

salt and pepper

If you like mulled wine, you'll love this cabbage.

Put all ingredients in a large saucepan, cover and cook gently for 1¼ hours, stirring occasionally.

◗ May be prepared the day before.

✳ May be frozen.

To re-heat – either put in a microwave on high for 7 minutes, stirring half way through, or put in the oven: 190°C, 375°F, Gas Mark 5 for 30 minutes.

Cook's tip: Pour out a third glass of red wine so that you can drink it while you eat the crisps!

FLAPJACK TART WITH APPLE, PECAN AND GINGER

110g (4oz) butter

3 tbsp golden syrup

3 tbsp brown sugar

225g (8oz) rolled oats

FILLING

2 tins or jars (350g each) chunky
apple purée or apple slices

2 heaped tbsp ginger conserve

50g (2oz) pecans

1 heaped tbsp brown sugar

Oven: 190°C, 375°F, Gas Mark 5

My son, Jack, helped me develop this recipe. He is very partial to flapjacks and when he was younger used to think they were just called "flaps" as when people offered them to him they would say "would you like a flap Jack".

To make the flapjack tart - you will need a greased flan tin, (preferably loose bottomed), 28cm (11") in diameter. Melt the butter in a saucepan, add golden syrup, sugar, oats and stir to coat. Spread into the flan tin and push up the sides of the tin to form the tart. Put in oven for 15 - 20 minutes until golden.

◗ May be prepared up to this stage the day before.

❉ May be frozen.

To make the filling - mix apple and ginger conserve together. Spread into flapjack base, add pecans and sprinkle brown sugar on top. Put back in oven for 15 minutes. May be served with Greek yoghurt or fromage frais.

Cook's tip: The easiest way to spread the flapjack mixture into the flan tin is with your fingers but be careful not to burn them on the hot mixture. The back of a spoon also works well.

ORDER OF PREPARATION IF MAKING IN ADVANCE:

The day before:
1. Make flapjack tart.
2. Make starter up to ◗
3. Make red cabbage.

In the evening:
4. Prepare and cook guinea fowl and barley.
5. Finish off starter and put in oven as needed.
6. Re-heat red cabbage.
7. Put filling in tart and put in oven as necessary.

ORDER OF PREPARATION IN UNDER 90 MINUTES:

1. Prepare and cook red cabbage.
2. Prepare and cook guinea fowl and barley.
3. Make flapjack tart and prepare filling.
4. Make starter.
5. Have a glass of wine and a packet of crisps.

FINGER FOOD IN A FLASH

Y New World Fizz.
Recommendation- Lindauer Brut
from New Zealand

"*C*anapes are too time consuming and people always eat more than you think at drinks parties." This is enough to put anyone off having a drinks party but don't despair, here are some ideas to make you change your mind. The following recipes are designed for speed and most can be prepared in advance. Presentation is all important. Food looks a lot better when it's spaced out rather than piled high on plates so arrange the food sparingly on platters and refill frequently. If you don't have enough platters, use trays which can be covered in silver foil or napkins.

MINI BAGELS WITH SMOKED SALMON AND CREAM CHEESE

3 bagels
100g (3½oz) cream cheese
100g (3½oz) smoked salmon
1 lemon
pepper

I once found a recipe for mini bagels but decided it would take a day or so to make them. My version is a lot quicker, look just as effective and are a perfect "bite-size".

Cut bagels vertically into slices or wedges (each bagel should produce around 12 slices). Spread each slice with cream cheese and put a small piece of smoked salmon on top. Squeeze the juice of half the lemon on top and sprinkle with freshly ground pepper. Cut remaining half lemon into thin slices. Put on a large platter and decorate with the lemon slices.

May be made up to 3 hours before serving. Cover with cling-film and keep chilled.

MEXICAN CRUDITÉS

8 spicy Mexican sausages
3 pepper pack (i.e. a red, yellow and green pepper)
1 large packet tortilla chips
DIPS
1 tub tomato salsa plus 1 handful chopped coriander
1 tub cheese and chive dip plus 1 handful chives chopped
1 tub guacamole plus 3 spring onions chopped

Crudités and dips are always a great stand-by as you can usually prepare them in advance and just leave them for people to help themselves. These Mexican crudités looks great with the three different coloured dips and the red, yellow and green peppers. The spiciness makes a pleasant change. However be warned, it might make your guests drink more!

Cook the sausages and allow to cool. De-seed and slice the peppers and keep in a polythene bag until needed. Mix the extra ingredient with each of the dips and put into ramekins or little bowls.

◑ May be prepared up to this stage the day before.

On a large platter, put dips in the middle and arrange sausages, pepper slices and tortilla chips around them.

Opposite: Instant Indian From The Store Cupboard (page 147)

PIZZA SQUARES WITH SPINACH AND CHÈVRE

2 large pizza bases (around 150g each) – stone baked recommended

1 tbsp olive oil

400g (14oz) frozen leaf spinach – de-frosted and drained

200g (7oz) chèvre

Oven: 220°C, 425°F, Gas Mark 7

I always think you need a bit of starch to soak up the alcohol at drinks parties and these are ideal.

Cut the pizza bases into approx. 4cm (1½") squares. Each pizza should produce around 26 pieces.

Put on a baking tray and brush with olive oil. Divide the spinach between the squares. Slice the chèvre or crumble it up and put on top.

❋ May be prepared earlier in the day.

Put in oven for 10 minutes.

Cook's tip: For an even speedier version, buy a couple of good quality pizzas, cut them into squares, add some sliced chèvre or other toppings, e.g. chorizo, black olives, prawns, and pop them in the oven.

MARINATED MOZZARELLA, CHERRY TOMATOES AND BLACK OLIVES

250g (9oz) small mozzarella balls – drained

350g (12oz) black olives – drained

300g (10½oz) cherry tomatoes

2 handfuls fresh chopped basil

1 tbsp olive oil

salt and pepper

 These three main ingredients look very colourful together and are ideal to leave in a bowl for people to pick at.

Mix all ingredients together. Serve with cocktail sticks.

◗ May be made up to two days in advance.

Cook's tip: If you can't find small mozzarella balls, then use the larger type cut into cubes.

SUN-DRIED TOMATO AND PUFF PASTRY PINWHEELS

1 packet (375g) ready-rolled puff pastry

½ jar (90g) sun-dried tomato paste

2 tbsp grated Parmesan

Oven: 220°C, 425°F, Gas Mark 7

 These pinwheels, which look a bit like mini Danish pastries, can be made in advance and re-heated.

Unroll pastry and spread the sun-dried tomato paste over it. Starting from the widest side, roll up tightly. Cut into about 30 slices, 1cm (½") thick, and put onto a baking tray and sprinkle grated Parmesan on top. Cook in oven for 10 minutes and serve hot.

◗ May be made the day before.

❋ May be frozen.

To re-heat – put back in oven for 5 minutes.

Opposite: Carefree Christmas (page 153)

BERRY BERRY PUNCH

250g (9oz) frozen raspberries

1 litre cranberry juice

3 bottles sparkling white wine – chilled

If you're fed up with mulled wine, tepid Chardonnay or some awful sickly fruit punch made with 90% lemonade, this punch will make a pleasant change. Using frozen raspberries will chill it down immediately so you won't need so much fridge space.

Put frozen raspberries and cranberry juice in a liquidizer or food processor to blend. Mix ⅓ of this mixture with each bottle of sparkling white wine.

Barman's tips: As it is likely to be cold around this time of the year, why not store the wine outside to chill it? This punch can also be made with other fruit, e.g. strawberries, blueberries, blackberries.

ORDER OF PREPARATION IF MAKING IN ADVANCE:

The day before:
1. Make marinated mozzarella, tomato and olives.
2. Make Mexican crudités.
3. Make pinwheels.

Earlier on the day:
3. Prepare pizza squares.

In the evening:
4. Make mini bagels.
5. Make berry berry punch.
6. Re-heat pinwheels and cook pizza.
7. Arrange Mexican crudités on platter.

ORDER OF PREPARATION IN UNDER 90 MINUTES:

1. Make marinated mozzarella, etc.
2. Make Mexican crudités.
3. Prepare pizza squares and put in oven as needed.
4. Make pinwheels and put in oven to cook as needed.
5. Make mini bagels.
6. Make berry berry punch and have a drink.

OTHER RECIPES TO SERVE AS FINGER FOOD:

Spicy Salsa and Red Leicester Mini Tarts (page 36)

Focaccia and Marinated Peppers, Olives and Anchovies (page 45)

Focaccia with Mascarpone and Sweet Onion Compote (page 48)

Oriental Hors d'oeuvre with Thai Dipping Sauces (page 51)

Mini Crispy Tarts with Pastrami and Dill Cucumber (page 60)

Asparagus in a Prosciutto Wrap (page 65)

Avocado and Red Kidney Bean Dip with Tortilla Chips (page 79)

Sweet Onion and Harissa Jam Tarts (page 82)

Mini Seafood Spring Rolls with a Sweet Chilli Sauce (page 85)

Polenta and Pesto Pizzas with Sun-dried Tomatoes and Gorgonzola (page 88)

Suburban Sushi (page 108)

Crostini with Smoked Venison (page 153)

GOOD GAME

⚱ *A full bodied, spicy red. Recommendation – d'Arenberg The Footbolt Old Vines Shiraz from Australia*

*M*y husband has been on a few shoots and each time I have hoped that he would return empty handed! If, like me, you like game but hate the thought of plucking, drawing, skinning and paunching, then this menu is for you. I have used ready-prepared "mixed game packs" and all you have to do is open the packet. If on the other hand you enjoy all the gory bits, then there's no reason why you shouldn't indulge.

BAKED CHÈVRE WITH LIME MARINATED SULTANAS ON MUFFINS

110g (4oz) sultanas
juice of 2 limes
4 tbsp walnut oil
1 tsp caster sugar
4 individual rounds of chèvre (100g each) – cut in half horizontally
4 muffins
1 bag (80g) lambs lettuce
salt and pepper
Oven: 190°C, 375°F, Gas Mark 5

❧ Thanks go to my great friend and continual source of inspiration, Rebecca, for this wonderful recipe.

Mix sultanas with lime juice, walnut oil, sugar, salt and pepper. Leave to marinate for at least 30 minutes or longer.

◗ May be prepared up to this stage the day before.

Cut muffins in half and put on a baking tray. Place chèvre rounds on top and put in oven for 10-15 minutes until the cheese begins to get "gungy".

Arrange lambs lettuce around the edge of each plate. Place muffin in middle and put marinated sultanas on top.

MIXED GAME CASSOULET WITH APPLES AND CIDER ****

This is not only an unusual way to serve cassoulet, but an unusual way to serve game and the combination works brilliantly. A lovely gamey (but not too gamey) cassoulet, slightly sweetened by cooking it in cider and giving it a different slant by using chick peas instead of haricot beans.

2 tbsp olive oil
1 large onion – chopped
2 garlic cloves – chopped
500g (1lb 2oz) venison sausages – cut into chunks
900g (2lbs) mixed game (see Cook's tip below)
2 tbsp plain flour
900ml (1½pts) cider
2 tins (400g each) chick peas
2 apples – cored and cut into chunks (no need to peel)
4 tbsp white breadcrumbs – made from 1 slice bread
2 handfuls chopped parsley
salt and pepper
Oven: 170°C, 325°F, Gas Mark 3

You will need a very large flame-proof casserole or large saucepan. Heat the oil, add the chopped onion and garlic and fry for 3 minutes. Add the chopped sausages, mixed game and flour and fry for a further 5 minutes, to brown the meat. Add cider gradually, while stirring, and bring up to the boil. If in a saucepan, transfer to a casserole dish, cover and put in oven for 1 ½ hours. After the first hour add the chick peas, chopped apple and season. Sprinkle the breadcrumbs on top and put back in oven, uncovered, for the last ½ hour. Sprinkle chopped parsley on top and serve. If making in advance, do not put breadcrumbs on top until re-heating.

◗ May be made the day before.

❋ May be frozen.

To re-heat – sprinkle breadcrumbs on top and put in oven: 190°C, 375°F, Gas Mark 5 for 45 minutes – 1 hour or until piping hot.

Cook's tip: Packets of mixed game are available from most major supermarkets. They normally come in packs of around 450g and contain pheasant, venison and various other game. If you cannot find them, you can use a mixture of pheasant breasts, venison and rabbit and cut them into chunks.

COUSCOUS

Most recipes for couscous will tell you to steam it over muslin – sounds like a real pain? Well, there's no need to, all you have to do is soak it in hot stock. Couscous goes extremely well with the cassoulet as it soaks up all the delicious juices and flavours.

400g (14oz) couscous
900ml (1½pts) chicken, beef or vegetable stock – made with one stock cube and boiling water
salt and pepper

Pour hot stock onto couscous and leave to soak for 10 minutes. Fork through the couscous to break up any lumps, season and serve.

COURGETTES WITH MUSTARD

1.5kg (3lbs 5oz) courgettes – sliced

2 tsp whole grain mustard

1 tbsp olive oil

salt and pepper

Plunge courgettes into boiling water and cook for 5 minutes. Drain, return to pan and toss in mustard, olive oil, salt and pepper.

Cook's tip: Courgettes tend to retain water in cooking so make sure you drain them very well.

STICKY TOFFEE BANANA MILLE-FEUILLE

1 packet (375g) ready-rolled
puff pastry

110g (4oz) toffee – or about
12 separate toffees

1 small pot (150g) ready-made custard

300ml (½pt) double cream

6 bananas

juice of ½ lemon

icing sugar for dusting

Oven: 190°C, 375°F, Gas Mark 5

 "Gooey", creamy, sticky toffee banana sandwiched between layers of light flakey pastry.

Unroll the pastry and cut into 8 squares. Put onto a baking tray and put in oven for 20 minutes until golden and puffed up. Meanwhile put the toffees and custard in a saucepan and melt gradually over a gentle heat, stirring from time to time. When the toffees have melted, take off the heat and allow to cool. Whisk cream and fold into the toffee mixture.

◗ May be prepared up to this stage the day before.

Slice the bananas, sprinkle with lemon juice and mix into toffee mixture. Cut the pastry squares in half horizontally. Place the bottom half on each serving plate. Pile the toffee bananas on top and finish off with the pastry top. Dust with icing sugar.

ORDER OF PREPARATION IF MAKING IN ADVANCE:

The day before.
1. Marinate sultanas.
2. Make cassoulet.
3. Make pudding up to ◗

In the evening:
4. Re-heat cassoulet.
5. Prepare starter and heat just before serving.
6. Make couscous.
7. Cook courgettes as needed.
8. Assemble mille-feuille.

ORDER OF PREPARATION IN UNDER 90 MINUTES:

1. Make cassoulet ****
2. Marinate sultanas and prepare starter.
3. Make mille-feuille.
4. Make couscous.
5. Cook courgettes.

CONSUMING PASSION

♀ *Champagne: Henri Harlin Brut N.V.*

This menu for Valentines Day has been designed to create an amorous mood using seductive food. What could be more romantic than hearts, intercourse, and double beds? I have given the quantities, as usual, for 8 people but if you want a "dinner a deux", then simply divide the quantities by 4.

PUFF PASTRY HEARTS WITH ASPARAGUS SPEARS IN HOLLANDAISE SAUCE

1 packet (375g) ready-rolled puff pastry

1kg (2lbs 4oz) fresh or frozen asparagus

1 jar (250ml) hollandaise sauce

Oven: 190°C, 375°F, Gas Mark 5

What better way can you think of to start a dinner than hearts and arrows? I have not only chosen asparagus for their spear (or arrow) appearance but also it is claimed to be an aphrodisiac.

Unroll pastry and cut out 8 heart shapes, as large as possible, by using a heart pastry cutter or making a template to cut round. Put on a baking tray and keep in fridge until needed to cook.

◐ May be prepared the day before.

Cook pastry hearts in oven for 20 minutes until golden and puffed up. If using fresh asparagus, cut the woody ends off, plunge into boiling water for 4-6 minutes until tender and drain. For frozen asparagus, cook as instructions on packet. Serve hollandaise sauce at room temperature poured over asparagus with the hearts laid on top to get "arrow in the heart" effect.

LEMON SORBET IN CHAMPAGNE

1 tub (500ml) lemon sorbet

1 bottle Champagne

A cooling intercourse to calm the passion until later.

Put a scoop of lemon sorbet into a champagne or wine glass. Pour champagne over sorbet slowly as it will froth up. Eat with spoons or use straws.

HERB STUFFED PLAICE

16 plaice fillets - skinned

200g (7oz) "Philadelphia" cream cheese

2 handfuls fresh chopped chives (reserve a few whole stems for decoration)

2 handfuls fresh chopped tarragon

juice 1 lemon

6 tbsp olive oil

salt and pepper

Oven: 190°C, 375°F, Gas Mark 5

Mix Philadelphia with half the chopped herbs. Spread mixture on plaice fillets and roll up starting at the widest end. Put in an oven-proof dish in one layer, pour the lemon juice on top, season and cover with foil. Mix remaining herbs with olive oil , salt and pepper.

◐ May be prepared up to this stage the day before.
Cook fish in oven for 30 minutes. Add the olive oil and herbs to the fish and mix together with cooking liquid (don't worry if it looks as if it's separating). Serve fish with juices and decorate with reserved chive stems on top.

Cook's tip: Even though this should be served on a double bed of red and yellow peppers, I would suggest serving it on a single bed of pasta beaus as the pasta soaks up the juices.

ROASTED RED AND YELLOW PEPPERS

3 red peppers – de-seeded and sliced

4 yellow peppers – de-seeded and sliced

2 large onions – thinly sliced

3 tbsp olive oil

salt and pepper

Oven: 190°C, 375°F, Gas Mark 5

Put all ingredients into a large roasting dish and toss in olive oil. Cook for 45 minutes, tossing occasionally.

PASTA BEAUS WITH PESTO

500g (1lb 2oz) Farfalle
(pasta bows or butterflies)

3 tbsp pesto

Cook as instructions on packet, drain and toss in pesto.

PASSION FRUIT AND PINEAPPLE SYLLABUB

300ml (½pt) double cream

4 tbsp icing sugar

4 tbsp rum

300g (10oz) Greek yoghurt

8 passion fruit

1 pineapple

This fruity refreshing syllabub, should be served "semi-freddo" (semi-frozen).

Put the cream in a large bowl with the icing sugar and rum. Whisk until thick and fold in the yoghurt. Cut 4 passion fruit in half and scoop the pulp into cream mixture along with half the pineapple, skinned and cut into very small chunks. Fold together and put into 8 ramekin dishes. Freeze for at least 30 minutes.

❋ May be kept in freezer for up to 2 months.

Take out of freezer 30 minutes before you are going to serve them. Cut the remaining passion fruit in half and slice the remaining pineapple. Serve fruit with the syllabub.

Cook's tip: If you still need more energy and have the room, end the meal with a cup of cocoa. Casanova used to have a cup of hot cocoa every night to give him energy for seducing. Alternatively serve coffee and chocolates.

ORDER OF PREPARATION IF MAKING IN ADVANCE:

The day before:
1. Make syllabub.
2. Cut out pastry hearts.
3. Prepare plaice up to

In the evening:
4. Cut up fruit and remember to take syllabub out of freezer 30 minutes before serving.
5. Roast peppers and cook fish and pasta as needed.
6. Put pastry hearts in oven and cook asparagus as needed.
7. Remember intercourse.

ORDER OF PREPARATION IN UNDER 90 MINUTES:

1. Prepare peppers and put in oven as needed.
2. Prepare fish and put in oven as needed.
3. Make syllabub and cut up fruit.
4. Prepare pastry hearts, put in oven and cook asparagus as needed.
5. Cook pasta.
6. Remember intercourse.

LOSING POUNDS WITH PANACHE

♀ An unoaked Chardonnay.
Recommendation – De Wetshof Bon
Vallon Special Reserve Chardonnay
from South Africa

*S*limming doesn't have to be boring and, even more important, you shouldn't have to feel deprived while everyone else is tucking into all the "goodies". This menu is devised to appeal to dieters and "skinnies" alike so that you'll be able to cook one meal that everyone will enjoy.

2 butternut squashes (total weight approx. 1kg (2lbs 4oz)) – peeled and de-seeded and cut into chunks

1 large potato – scrubbed and cut into chunks

1 large onion – chopped

1.5 litres (2¾pts) vegetable or chicken stock – made from 3 stock cubes and boiling water

2 oranges – zest and juice

1 bunch chives – snipped

salt and pepper

BUTTERNUT SQUASH AND ORANGE SOUP

I'm so pleased that people have become more aware of squashes and that they are getting more and more popular over here. A few years ago, when I asked in a supermarket if they had butternut squash, I was directed to the orange squash! Out of all the different types of squash, the butternut is my favourite as it has a lovely smooth mellow flavour.

Put all ingredients, except the chives, in a large saucepan. Bring up to the boil and simmer for 20 minutes until vegetables are soft. Put in a liquidizer or food processor to blend.

◑ May be prepared the day before.

❋ May be frozen.

To re-heat – put in a saucepan and heat gently until piping hot. Pour into bowls and decorate with snipped chives. May be served with warm bread or rolls – see Handy Hints page 11.

Cook's tip: If the soup becomes too thick once re-heated, add some more stock or skimmed milk to thin it down a little.

TURKEY, MUSHROOM AND RED PEPPER STROGOULASH

2 onions – thinly sliced

3 garlic cloves - crushed

1 litre (1¾pts) passatta or creamed tomatoes

900g (2lbs) turkey steaks or fillets – cut into strips (see Cook's tip below)

2 red peppers – de-seeded and sliced

250g (9oz) chestnut mushrooms – sliced

4 tsp caraway seeds

1 tbsp paprika plus some for sprinkling on top

salt

1 tub (200g) Greek yoghurt

I couldn't decide whether to make this a stroganoff or goulash so I combined them both to create this lovely, colourful warming dish.

Put onions, garlic, and passatta/creamed tomatoes in a large saucepan, bring up to boil then allow to simmer for 15 minutes. Add the turkey, red peppers, mushrooms and caraway seeds and continue to cook for a further 15 minutes. Season with paprika and salt.

◑ May be prepared the day before.

To re-heat – return to the saucepan and heat gently for about 10 minutes, until hot through.

To serve – put a blob of Greek yoghurt on top of each portion when serving and finish off with a sprinkling of paprika.

Cook's tip: Some supermarkets sell turkey in strips for stir-frying which would be ideal for this recipe.

GREEN HERBED BULGUR WHEAT

500g (1lb 2oz) bulgur wheat

1.2 litres (2pts) chicken or vegetable stock – made from 2 stock cubes and boiling water

1 bunch spring onions – finely sliced

2 handfuls chopped basil

2 handfuls chopped parsley

salt and pepper

 This lovely, fluffy, nutty grain makes a pleasant change from rice or potatoes.

Put the bulgur wheat in a saucepan with the stock, bring up to boil and simmer for 10 minutes or until liquid has been absorbed. Add all other ingredients and serve.

BALSAMIC LEEKS WITH WHOLEGRAIN MUSTARD

8 large leeks

2 tbsp balsamic vinegar

2 tsp wholegrain mustard

salt and pepper

This recipe shows that you don't need to dowse vegetables in butter or oil. The addition of just a small amount of balsamic vinegar and mustard brings out the mild onion flavour in the leeks.

Thickly slice the leeks. Plunge into boiling water for 5 minutes and drain well. Return to the pan and toss together with vinegar, mustard, salt and pepper.

Cook's tip: Leeks tend to retain water so it is very important that they are drained well. Push them down into a colander with the back of a spoon to squeeze out the moisture.

HOT RASPBERRY RAMEKINS

3 eggs

4 tbsp "Canderell" or other artificial sweetener

3 tbsp plain flour

750g (1lb 10oz) "light" or ordinary fromage frais

500g (1lb 2oz) frozen raspberries

Oven: 180°C, 350°F, Gas Mark 4

A lovely creamy pudding – who would ever believe it's so low in calories?

Break eggs into a large bowl and beat in flour, artificial sweetener and fromage frais. Fold in frozen raspberries and put in ramekin dishes.

☼ May be prepared up to this stage earlier in the day.

Put in oven for 20 minutes and serve.

Cook's tip: Other fruits may be used, fresh or frozen e.g. blackberries, blackcurrants, mixed summer fruit.

ORDER OF PREPARATION IF MAKING IN ADVANCE:

The day before:
1. Make soup.
2. Make turkey strogoulash.

Earlier on the day:
3. Prepare fruit ramekins up to ☼

In the evening:
4. Re-heat soup and turkey.
5. Cook bulgur wheat and leeks as needed.
6. Put ramekins in oven as needed.

ORDER OF PREPARATION IN UNDER 90 MINUTES:

1. Prepare fruit ramekins and cook as needed.
2. Make soup and re-heat if necessary.
3. Make turkey strogoulash.
4. Cook bulgur wheat and leeks as needed.

INSTANT INDIAN FROM THE STORE CUPBOARD

♀ *A ripe, spicy white.*
Recommendation – Fetzer
Gewürztraminer from California

In a spontaneous mood, have you ever invited people over for dinner and hardly left yourself enough time to cook, let alone shop? If the answer is yes, then here is a complete menu which can be made entirely from ingredients in a store cupboard and freezer. If the answer is no, you still might want to save a visit to the shops when you don't feel like it and cook this menu anyway. The ingredients may not be those you just happen to have hanging around but next time you go shopping, why not buy the ingredients and store them for that next occasion.

SPICY RED LENTIL SOUP WITH POPPADOMS

2 tbsp olive oil
1 onion – chopped
350g (12oz) red lentils
4 tbsp tomato purée
2 tsp cumin seeds or powder
3 tsp curry powder
2 litres (3½pts) chicken or vegetable stock (using 2 stock cubes and boiling water)
1 packet mini poppadoms

Unlike other pulses, lentils need no soaking and can be cooked quickly – only 20 minutes in this recipe. I have used red lentils for two reasons, firstly because they cook down to form a purée which is ideal for soups and secondly for their wonderful colour. The addition of the spices make this soup a lovely warming way to start the meal.

Heat oil in a large saucepan, add chopped onion and fry gently for 5 minutes until golden. Add all other ingredients, bring up to boil and simmer for 20 minutes, stirring occasionally. Put in a liquidizer or food processor to blend.

◑ May be made the day before.

❄ May be frozen.

To re-heat – put back in saucepan over a gentle heat until piping hot. Serve with mini poppadoms.

Cook's tip: If you happen to have any yoghurt, it looks good swirled on top of the soup.

PRAWN, COD AND CHICK PEA MASALA

400g (14oz) large frozen prawns – de-frosted

2 tins (400g each) chick peas – drained

1 tin (400ml) coconut milk

1 jar (350g) "Tilda Madhur Jaffrey" Green Lime Masala or other similar type of "cook in" sauce

4 tsp coriander – preserved in jars (or fresh)

8 frozen cod portions (approx. 100g (3½oz) each)

salt and pepper

Oven: 190°C, 375°F, Gas Mark 5

This is a real cheat, ever so quick, tastes great and no one would believe what went into it. The "Green Lime Masala" sauce is described as "medium" but if you prefer a less spicy flavour, then use one of the "mild" sauces such as " Shahi Tandoori Sauce".

First de-frost the prawns (see Cook's tip below). Mix all other ingredients together (there is no need to de-frost the cod) and put in one layer in an oven-proof serving dish. Put in oven for 30 minutes. Add prawns and return to oven for a further 10 minutes.

Cook's tip: To help prawns de-frost quickly, put in a sieve and run under cold water.

LEMON AND SAFFRON RICE

400g (14oz) basmati or long grain rice

½ tsp saffron

zest and juice of 1 lemon or 4 tbsp "Jiff" lemon juice

salt and pepper

Saffron is one of the most expensive spices in the world. It comes from the stigma of the crocus and takes up to a quarter of a million flowers to make 500g (1lb) of saffron. Saffron used to grow in England around Saffron Walden, hence the name. Saffron is popular in Indian cooking and combines perfectly with rice giving a lovely fragrant, slightly bitter taste and golden yellow colour.

Bring 1 litre (1¾pts) salted water to the boil. Take off the heat, add saffron and leave to infuse for 10 minutes. Add rice, bring back up to boil and simmer for 15 minutes or until tender and liquid has been absorbed. Add lemon and check seasoning.

SPINACH WITH TOMATO, GINGER AND CUMIN

1.5kg (3lbs 5oz) frozen leaf spinach

1 tin (400g) chopped tomatoes

2 tsp ground ginger

3 tsp cumin – seeds or ground

salt and pepper

Store cupboard and freezer vegetables can lose their crunch after freezing/canning, but the two vegetables that I use as much frozen as fresh are peas and spinach. I love fresh spinach, especially in salads, but when cooking for large quantities, you need literally piles of it to get anywhere near the right amount. This is where frozen spinach comes in handy. Spinach, known as "saag" is very popular in Indian cooking, particularly with the addition of various spices.

Cook spinach in a saucepan as instructions on packet. Drain well and add other ingredients. Return to heat for 5 minutes and serve.

MANGO AND CARDAMOM KULFI WITH PISTACHIO NUTS AND CINNAMON

1 tin (400g) condensed milk

1 tin (400g) evaporated milk

2 tbsp caster sugar

3 tsp cinnamon

1 tbsp cardamom pods

2 tins (400g each) sliced mango – drained

100g (3½oz) shelled pistachio nuts – roughly chopped

This is a variation of a classic Indian dessert – a spiced mango ice cream. It's a lovely refreshing way to finish the meal and as good as any Italian ice creams I have eaten. It takes about 2 hours to freeze so I would suggest making it when you have a spare moment so that it's ready in the freezer to serve at any time when you're feeling spontaneous (alternatively see Cook's tip below).

Put condensed, evaporated milk and sugar in a saucepan, with 1 tsp cinnamon and cardamom pods. Bring up to boil, stirring frequently and then simmer for 5 minutes. Take off heat, and allow to cool slightly. Strain into a food processor and add drained mango slices. Blend until smooth. Line a Swiss roll tin with cling-film and pour mixture in. Leave to cool completely and then put in freezer for at least 2 hours.

❄ May be kept in a freezer for up to 3 months.

To serve – turn out of tin and remove cling-film. Cut into 8 rectangles and cut each rectangle into 2 triangles. Place 2 triangles on each plate, slightly over-lapping, and sprinkle remaining cinnamon and chopped pistachios on top.

Cook's tip: If you haven't already made the kulfi and you don't have time to wait 2 hours for it to freeze, then buy 1 litre of mango sorbet (available from most supermarkets) instead. Serve it in scoops with the cinnamon and pistachio nuts.

ORDER OF PREPARATION IF MAKING IN ADVANCE:

The day before:
1. Make kulfi.
2. Make soup.
3. De-frost prawns.

In the evening:
4. Prepare fish Masala and cook as needed (don't add frozen cod until just before going in oven).
5. Cook rice.
6. Cook spinach.
7. Re-heat soup.

ORDER OF PREPARATION IN UNDER 90 MINUTES:

1. Make kulfi **** or buy mango sorbet.
2. De-frost prawns and prepare Masala, adding frozen cod just before putting in oven.
3. Make soup.
4. Cook rice.
5. Cook spinach.

THANK GOODNESS IT'S NOT TURKEY

♀ *A fruity New World Grenache. Recommendation – Peter Lehmann Vine Vale Grenache from Australia*

*E*ven though I love turkey, after the build up to Christmas with all the office parties and other events, I'm often fed up with it before Christmas day arrives. If you also feel you have "overdosed" on turkey, here's the ideal menu to ring the changes.

SMOKED HADDOCK AND LEEK TIMBALES WITH A LEMON AND CHIVE DRESSING

oil – for greasing
700g (1lb 9oz) smoked haddock – skin and bones removed
2 leeks
1 tub (250g) fromage frais
2 eggs (medium sized)
1 bag (75g) watercress
pepper
LEMON AND CHIVE DRESSING
2 tbsp fromage frais
4 tbsp olive oil
juice of ½ lemon
1 packet fresh chives - chopped
salt and pepper
Oven: 190°C, 375°F, Gas Mark 5

A timbale is a high-sided mould and the preparation cooked inside it. If you don't have timbale moulds, there is no need to rush out and buy them, as ramekin dishes work just as well. This starter never fails to impress and is so easy to make – no need for a *bain-marie* or anything as technical as that! I prefer to use the undyed smoked haddock – not only is it healthier but I also prefer the colour of the finished product.

Brush 8 ramekin dishes or timbales with oil. Cut haddock and leeks into large chunks and put into food processor with all remaining ingredients, except watercress, to blend. Put into oiled ramekins/timbales and put in oven for 20 minutes. Mix all dressing ingredients together. If serving immediately, slide a flat knife round the sides of each ramekin, turn out on to individual plates and serve with watercress and dressing drizzled on top. If making in advance, leave in ramekins to cool.

◑ May be made up to this point the day before.

❋ The timbales may be frozen.

To re-heat – turn out of ramekins/timbales and put on an oiled baking tray in the oven for 10 - 15 minutes.

Serve with watercress and dressing as above. Serve with warm crusty bread - see Handy Hints page 11.

Cook's tip: Instead of making the dressing yourself, you can always use a ready made dressing such as "Waitrose Lemon Garlic and Chive Dressing" and use the chopped chives to sprinkle on top.

ROAST GAMMON WITH KUMQUATS AND A HONEY, MUSTARD AND SOY GLAZE ****

It's a great advantage that you can now buy "ready to bake" gammon, otherwise we would have to start making this recipe at least 24 hours earlier to allow it to soak and boil first. Instead, all you have to do is "bung"

2kg (4lbs 8oz) unsmoked gammon joint
4 tbsp wholegrain mustard
4 tbsp honey
4 tbsp dark soy sauce
300ml (½pt) orange juice
16 kumquats - sliced
Oven: 180°C, 350°F, Gas Mark 4

it in the oven. Kumquats look like little oranges and people either love or hate them. The skin is sweet and the flesh is sour and I personally love to eat them whole and enjoy the bitter sweetness. In this recipe they are sliced and cooked with honey and orange juice which sweetens and gives them a completely different taste. Those people who say they hate them, may be eating their words.

With a sharp knife, remove rind from gammon and wrap in foil. Make the glaze by mixing together half the mustard, honey and soy sauce. Mix remainder of mustard, honey and soy sauce together with the orange juice and kumquats. Keep refrigerated.

◖ May be prepared up to this point the day before.

Cook in oven for 2½ hours. For the last ½ hour of cooking, remove the foil, brush over the glaze and turn the oven up to 200°C, 400°F, Gas Mark 6.

Meanwhile heat the sauce in a saucepan and allow to simmer for 10 minutes.

Cook's tip: Kumquats are sometimes quite pippy. Remove the larger ones but don't worry about leaving some in as they add good roughage to the dish!

PUY LENTILS WITH RED ONION

1 tbsp olive oil
2 red onions – sliced
350g (12oz) Puy lentils or large green lentils
2 cartons (284ml each) chicken or vegetable stock or use 600ml (1pt) boiling water and 1 stock cube
salt and pepper

These tiny grey/green lentils are from Puy in France. They keep their shape and colour and have a more crunchy texture than other types of lentil. If Puy lentils are not available, then dried large green lentils work almost as well.

Put oil in a saucepan, add onions and fry gently for 5 minutes until softened and browned. Add lentils and stir into onions, continuing to cook for 1 minute. Add stock and bring up to the boil. Simmer Puy lentils gently for 35 minutes (green lentils only need 20 minutes) and season.

◖ May be prepared the day before.

To re-heat – put in microwave on high for 5 minutes.

Cook's tip: If making in advance, the lentils can be re-heated in the dish in which they are going to be served to save washing up.

CELERY AND HAZELNUT CRUMBLE

2 heads of celery
2 tubs (300-350g each) fresh cheese sauce
4 slices brown bread or 100g (3½oz) brown breadcrumbs
1 packet (100g) hazelnuts
paprika
Oven: 200°C, 400°F, Gas Mark 6

Celery is a vegetable that a lot of people forget can be cooked. So I have devised this recipe where it needs no blanching or braising so that it retains much of its crunch. The hazelnuts help bring out the naturally nutty flavour of the celery.

Trim the base of the celery, wash and slice. Put into a large oven-proof gratin dish and mix with cheese sauce. Put slices of brown bread and hazelnuts in a food processor to form crumbs. Scatter crumbs over celery mixture and sprinkle paprika on top.

◖ May be prepared up to this point the day before.

Put in oven, uncovered, for 30 - 40 minutes until piping hot and golden brown on top.

Cook's tip: If ever you have left-over stale bread, put it in a food processor to make breadcrumbs and keep in the freezer until needed.

CLAFOUTIS WITH CHERRIES IN KIRSCH WITH WHITE CHOCOLATE ICE CREAM

2 tins (425g each) pitted black cherries

large slug (approx 4 tbsp) kirsch

2 tbsp cornflour

8 ready-baked, frozen Yorkshire puddings

icing sugar for dusting

1litre white chocolate ice cream

Clafoutis is a dessert from the Limousin region of France consisting of black cherries covered with a thick pancake batter and a dusting of icing sugar. I have adapted this classic French recipe to turn it into an instant dessert.

Put the cherries, with juice, Kirsch and cornflour in a saucepan and bring up to the boil. Allow to simmer for a few minutes until thickened.

◖ May be prepared up to this point the day before.

Cook Yorkshire puddings according to instruction. Re-heat cherry mixture over a gentle heat for 5 minutes to warm. Fill Yorkshire puddings with cherries and dust generously with icing sugar. Serve warm with a scoop of ice cream.

ORDER OF PREPARATION IF MAKING IN ADVANCE:

The day before:
1. Prepare celery crumble up to ◖ but don't worry about washing food processor before processing timbales.
2. Make timbales up to ◖
3. Prepare gammon up to ◖
4. Prepare lentils up to ◖
5. Cook cherries with kirsch and turn ice cream into serving bowl.

In the evening:
1. Put gammon in oven, baste after 2 hours and heat sauce as necessary.
2. Put celery in oven as necessary.
3. Re-heat timbales.
4. Re-heat lentils.
5. Put Yorkshire puddings in oven and heat cherries as needed.

ORDER OF PREPARATION IN UNDER 90 MINUTES:

1. Prepare and cook gammon.
2. Prepare celery crumble and put in oven as needed.
3. Make timbales and cook as needed.
4. Cook lentils as needed.
5. Make pudding.

CAREFREE CHRISTMAS

♀ A California Zinfandel.
Recommendation – Franciscan
Oakville Zinfandel

*C*hristmas is a day that kids always look forward to but some adults dread. A whole day tied to the kitchen when you dream of being able to lie in, open presents leisurely, go for a walk, have a drink with friends, then come back to "stick a few things in the oven" before lunch. Well now your dream can come true, as all the recipes in this menu can be prepared the day before, allowing you to actually enjoy Christmas.

CROSTINI WITH SMOKED WILD VENISON

12 slices granary bread –
medium sliced

2 tbsp olive oil

250g (9oz) fromage frais

1 bunch chives (approx 3 tbsp) –
snipped

100g (3½oz) smoked wild venison –
(see Cook's tip below) sliced

salt and pepper

a few holly leaves

Oven: 200°C, 400°F, Gas Mark 6

This is an ideal starter for Christmas day as it can be served on a platter to eat with drinks, so that you can save on extra crockery and cutlery and cut down on washing up. It makes an unusual change from the normal type of Christmas starters and is also light and healthy, leaving room for you to "stuff" yourself afterwards!. Venison is low in fat, calories and cholesterol and I have used fromage frais which is also good for you.

Using a round pastry cutter (about 6cm/2½" in diameter), cut two circles of bread out of each slice. Reserve crusts for stuffing – see turkey recipe below. Put on a baking tray, brush with oil and put in oven for 10 minutes until golden. Mix fromage frais with 2 tbsp of the snipped chives, salt and pepper.

◗ May be prepared the day before.

❅ The crostini may be frozen.

Put a teaspoon of fromage frais mixture on each crostini. Lay the venison slices on top and sprinkle with remaining chives. Put on a platter and decorate with holly leaves. These may be prepared up to 2 hours before serving.

Cook's tips: Smoked wild venison is available from major supermarkets or by mail order from Cervina Ltd., The Stable Courtyard, Loseley Park, Guildford, Surrey, GU3 1HS. If freezing the crostini, there is no need to de-frost them first as they thaw very quickly and will help to keep the fromage frais cold.

CRANBERRY STUFFED TURKEY FILLETS WRAPPED IN BACON WITH A STILTON SAUCE

8 tbsp breadcrumbs (made from bread left over from crostini)

1 jar (180g) cranberry sauce

25g (1oz) softened butter or "Olivio"

8 turkey steaks – approx 1.2kg (2lbs 12oz) in total (see Cook's tip below)

16 rashers streaky rindless bacon

100g (3½oz) Stilton

300ml (½pt) red wine

1 tub (200ml) crème fraîche

pepper

Oven: 190°C, 375°F, Gas Mark 5

With this recipe there's no need to set your alarm for 6am to put your turkey in the oven. You can prepare it the day before and all you have to remember (after a few mulled wines) is to put it in the oven for 40 minutes.

Make breadcrumbs by putting left over crusts from crostini in a food processor. Take 8 tablespoons out to make stuffing and put the rest in the freezer to use on another occasion. Mix breadcrumbs with half the jar of cranberry sauce and the butter or "Olivio". Using a rolling pin, bash the turkey steaks to flatten them, divide the stuffing mixture between them and roll up. Wrap each stuffed turkey steak in 2 rashers of bacon so that it is virtually covered by the bacon with the overlapping bits at the bottom. Crumble up the Stilton and mix with wine, crème fraîche, remaining half jar of cranberry sauce and pepper. Put in a non-metallic dish and add turkey. Cover with foil.

◑ May be prepared up to this stage the day before.

Put turkey in a roasting or oven-proof dish, cover with foil and put in oven for 20 minutes. Remove the foil, baste, turn oven up to 200°C, 400°F, Gas Mark 6 and cook for a further 20 minutes.

To serve – slice turkey, fan out on each plate and spoon sauce over.

Cook's tips: Turkey steaks are available from major supermarkets. They do vary in size and if they are very small, you may need to allow 2 per person. If so, wrap one piece of bacon around each. If you find it too much trouble to slice the turkey, then just leave them whole.

CARROT, PARSNIP AND GINGER PURÉE

800g (1lb 12oz) carrots

800g (1lb 12oz) parsnips

2 handfuls fresh parsley

2 tsp ground ginger

1tsp granulated sugar

3 tbsp olive oil

salt and pepper

I hate having to stand over steaming pans of vegetables cooking at the last minute - not only do I object to missing out on a glass of champagne with my guests, but the steam makes my hair frizz! This purée can be frozen or prepared the day before and all you have to do is heat it up.

Peel and thickly slice carrots and parsnips. Plunge into boiling water, cook for 20 minutes or until very soft and drain well. Put half the parsley in a food processor to chop. Add carrots, parsnips, ginger, sugar, olive oil, salt and pepper to the food processor to blend.

◑ May be made the day before.

❄ May be frozen.

To re-heat – either microwave on high for 6 minutes, stirring half way through, or cover with foil and put in oven: 200°C, 400°F, Gas Mark 6 for 20 minutes. Chop remaining parsley and sprinkle on top.

Cook's tips: To save time, you can buy ready peeled and cut carrots and parsnips. If you have any purée left over, it will turn into wonderful soup by just adding some stock.

POTATO AND ONION CAKE

3 packets long life potato with onion and bacon

2 eggs – beaten

Oven: 200°C, 400°F, Gas Mark 6

This is a real cheat but so quick and simple. It looks really impressive served as a "cake". Don't be put off by the name of these potatoes as they are called "Farmhouse Brunch", "Country Supper" or something similar.

Grease a cake tin approx 24cm (9½") in diameter and line the base with baking parchment. Mix potatoes with beaten eggs and put into cake tin. Cook in oven for 35 minutes.

◑ May be prepared up to this stage the day before.

Turn potatoes out onto an oven-proof serving plate and put back in oven for 15 minutes to brown the top.

Cook's tips:. If you prefer, this can be cooked in individual ramekin dishes lined with baking parchment and turned out as above or it can be cooked and served in a large gratin dish which will need only 35 minutes cooking in total.

CHRISTMAS ROULADE WITH A BRANDY MAC SAUCE

5 eggs

1 jar (410g) good quality mincemeat

1 tub (200g) Greek yoghurt

2 tbsp icing sugar

BRANDY MAC SAUCE

1 tub (400ml) custard – preferably fresh

slug of brandy (approx 2 tbsp)

slug of ginger wine (approx 2 tbsp)

Oven: 190°C, 375°F, Gas Mark 5

This roulade is a refreshing change from Christmas pudding and as it resembles a log, still looks festive. As some people have a fear of making roulades, I got Katie, my 8 year old daughter to test this recipe. She did everything, weighed out the ingredients, mixed, whisked, cooked, rolled and it turned out perfectly. If an 8 year old can do it, then you've got no excuse!

Grease a roulade tin and line with baking parchment. Separate the eggs and mix the yolks with mincemeat. Whisk whites until stiff and fold into mincemeat and yolks. Put into roulade tin, smooth mixture level with a palate knife and cook in oven for 13 minutes. Leave to cool in the tin.

Turn roulade out of tin onto foil. Mix Greek yoghurt with 1 tbsp of icing sugar and spread over roulade. Using the foil to help, roll the roulade.

To make sauce – mix custard with brandy and ginger wine.

◗ May be prepared the day before.

✳ The roulade may be frozen.

To serve – unwrap roulade and, using the foil to help, lift onto a serving plate. Dust with remaining 1 tbsp icing sugar. Slice and serve with Brandy Mac sauce.

Cook's tip: This recipe is easier to make after you have had a Brandy Mac to drink!

ORDER OF PREPARATION IF MAKING IN ADVANCE:

1. Make roulade and Brandy Mac sauce.
2. Make starter up to ◗
3. Prepare potatoes up to ◗
4. Prepare turkey up to ◗
5. Make carrot and parsnip purée.

On the day:
6. Assemble starter.
7. Put turkey in oven.
8. Re-heat purée and potatoes.

ORDER OF PREPARATION IN UNDER 90 MINUTES:

1. Make roulade and Brandy Mac sauce.
2. Prepare potatoes and cook as needed.
3. Prepare turkey and cook as needed.
4. Make starter.
5. Make carrot and parsnip purée.

CHRISTMAS LEFT-OVERS

♀ A light red. Recommendation –
Redwood Trail, Pinot Noir from
California. A lightly oaked white.
Recommendation – Casa Porta
Chardonnay from Chile.

*I*t's the day after Boxing Day, you've got a fridge full of left-overs and
you're not sure what to do with them. Well here is the perfect solution.

PEAR, CELERY AND WALNUT SALAD WITH
A WARM STILTON DRESSING

 This is a lovely light, refreshing salad to use up your left-over Stilton
and any kind of nuts.

4 pears - cored and sliced but not peeled
juice ½ lemon
4 sticks celery – sliced
100g (3½oz) nuts – any kind
100g (3½oz) crisp leaves – shredded
DRESSING
115g (4oz) Stilton
100ml crème fraîche
3 tbsp milk
pepper

Put sliced pears in a large salad bowl and mix with lemon juice. Add sliced
celery, nuts and shredded leaves. Put all dressing ingredients into a saucepan
and heat gently until Stilton has dissolved. Pour over salad, toss and serve.
May be served with warm bread or rolls – see Handy Hints page 6.

*Cook's tip: Choose leaves which will remain crisp after a few days in the fridge, e.g.
iceberg or gem lettuce, Chinese cabbage. The pears may be replaced by apples or
dried pears.*

LEFT-OVERS WITH A MUSHROOM SAUCE
IN PUFF PASTRY CASES

 This recipe will help use up the cold turkey and all the trimmings. It's
a kind of "posh" version of a turkey pie and is sure to impress.

800g (1lb 12oz) left-over cooked turkey, bacon, sausage, stuffing etc.
1 tin (400g) artichoke hearts – drained and cut in half
200g (7oz) mushrooms – sliced
2 cans "Campbell's Condensed Cream of Mushroom Soup"
1 large glass of white wine (approx 200ml/ ⅓ pt)
1 packet (375g) ready-rolled puff pastry
1 egg – beaten
pepper
Oven: 200°C, 400°F, Gas Mark 6

Slice or chop turkey, bacon, etc. Mix with artichokes, mushrooms, soup, wine
and pepper. Put in an oven-proof casserole and cover.
To make puff pastry cases – unroll pastry and cut into 8 squares. With a sharp
knife mark the surface of the squares with a diamond pattern. Put on a
baking tray and brush with beaten egg (reserve remaining egg for the bubble
and squeak cakes).

◑ May be prepared up to this stage the day before.

Put turkey in oven for 45 minutes or until piping hot, stirring half way through
cooking. Put pastry squares in oven for 20 minutes until golden and puffed
up. Cut pastry squares in half horizontally, place bottom half on each serving
plate, divide the turkey mixture between them and put the top back on.

BUBBLE AND SQUEAK CAKES

 Bubble and squeak – ideal for left-overs and has now become extremely trendy.

700g (1lb 9oz) left-over potatoes
600g (1lb 5oz) left-over vegetables
25g (1oz) butter or "Olivio"
left-over egg (from recipe above)
salt and pepper
Oven: 200°C, 400°F, Gas Mark 6

Grease a baking tray. Either put all ingredients in a food processor and put on pulse for a few seconds to amalgamate but leave coarse, or chop and mix together. With your hands, form into 16 cakes and put on to baking tray.

◗ May be prepared the day before.

Cook in oven for 20 minutes turning half way though.

Cook's tip: If you don't have enough left-over potatoes, just boil some more to make up to the correct quantity.

CARROTS IN HONEY AND CINNAMON

 Deliciously sweet and slightly spicy.

1.5kg (3lbs 5oz) carrots – sliced
2 tbsp honey
1 tsp ground cinnamon
salt and pepper

Plunge carrots into boiling water and cook for about 8 minutes until almost tender but still crisp. Drain, return to pan and toss together with other ingredients.

Cook's tip: No carrots, then just use whatever vegetables you have in your freezer.

CHRISTMAS PUDDING SYLLABUB WITH BISCOTTI

The only way to describe this creamy syllabub is rich and luscious. It looks especially good when served in individual ramekin dishes. It's delicious served with Cantuccini Biscotti, a very crisp Italian biscuit with almonds which are great to eat dipped into dessert wine or coffee.

250g (7oz) Christmas pudding or cake – crumbled
1 carton (400ml) custard (preferably fresh)
large slug brandy (approx 4 tbsp or more)
1 small pineapple – cut into small chunks
300ml (½pt) double cream – whisked
1 packet Cantuccini Biscotti (or other crisp biscuits may be used)

Mix the crumbled Christmas cake with custard, brandy and pineapple. Fold in the whisked cream and put in ramekin dishes or one big dish. Chill for at least 30 minutes.

◗ May be made the day before.

Serve with Cantuccini Biscotti.

ORDER OF PREPARATION IN UNDER 90 MINUTES:

1. Make syllabub.
2. Prepare turkey recipe and cook as needed.
3. Prepare bubble and squeak cakes and cook as needed.
4. Prepare carrots and cook as needed.
5. Make salad.

INDEX